John I. Goodlad
Corinne Mantle-Bromley
Stephen John Goodlad

Education for Everyone

Agenda for Education
in a Democracy

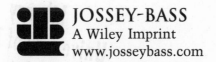

JOSSEY-BASS
A Wiley Imprint
www.josseybass.com

Published by Jossey-Bass
A Wiley Imprint
989 Market Street, San Francisco, CA 94103-1741   www.josseybass.com

Jossey-Bass books and products are available through most bookstores. To contact Jossey-Bass directly call our Customer Care Department within the U.S. at 800-956-7739, outside the U.S. at 317-572-3986, or fax 317-572-4002.

Jossey-Bass also publishes its books in a variety of electronic formats. Some content that appears in print may not be available in electronic books.

ISBN: 0–7879–7224–X

Library of Congress Cataloging-in-Publication Data

Goodlad, John I.
  Education for everyone : agenda for education in a democracy.-- 1st ed.
       p. cm. -- (The Jossey-Bass education series)
Written by John I. Goodlad, Corinne Mantle-Bromley, Stephen John Goodlad.
Includes bibliographical references and index.
  ISBN 0-7879-7224-X (alk. paper)
  1. Education--Aims and objectives--United States. 2. Democracy--Study and teaching--United States. 3. Educational equalization--United States. I. Mantle-Bromley, Corinne. II. Goodlad, Stephen John. III. Title. IV. Series.
  LA217.2.G663 2004
  370.11'5'0973--dc22
                                    2003026852

Printed in the United States of America
FIRST EDITION
HB Printing   10 9 8 7 6 5 4 3 2 1

The Jossey-Bass Education Series

Contents

Preface

For some time—increasingly since World War II—too many of us occupying this richly endowed part of the world have assumed that the work-in-progress we call democracy will take care of us. This is a dangerous assumption. Things thought not to need our caring attention deteriorate.

Early leaders of the republic were aware of this. They saw education as providing for all citizens the necessary apprenticeship in the understanding and practice of democracy. It has taken centuries to expand "all citizens" to really include everyone—and such inclusion has a long way to go in providing a rich and meaningful apprenticeship to all people. During this lengthy process, the study and practice of democracy in our schools has weakened. We must return to the primary purpose of education while ensuring that it is indeed for everyone.

To make democracy safe, we must have universal schooling; to make this schooling safe for education, we must have democracy. Whether we are or are not professional educators, each of us shares responsibility for taking care of democracy by ensuring education for responsible citizenship. We hope that this book will assist you in your fulfillment of the most patriotic service one can provide.

The idea of writing this book evolved as more and more people both inside and outside the field of education requested comprehensive but brief summaries of the Agenda for Education in a Democracy—an agenda shared by colleagues at the Institute for Educational Inquiry, at the Center for Educational Renewal, and across the country in member settings of the National Network for

Educational Renewal. Many people engaged us in conversation pertaining to its genesis and justification. There was a flurry of such interest following the horrors of September 11, 2001, and the subsequent worldwide shock and intense preoccupation with the question "Why?" The ensuing debate has been intense and much of it has been over balancing the tenets of freedom and liberty with the restrictions necessary for our protection from terrorism.

In responding to the wide range of requests that came primarily to us at the Institute for Educational Inquiry, staff members found it necessary to tailor-make most of our responses. No one short document sufficed. When the questions were complex, which most were, we rather lamely suggested the reading of this or that volume among some seventeen books written over the past twenty years, no one of which embraces the whole of what we were asked. We decided to write a book that would be a reasonably comprehensive source for persons wanting to understand the Agenda for Education in a Democracy and the premises on which it is based—but not a yearlong curriculum of study.

Our intended audience is, then, people—educators and others—who already know something about the Agenda for Education in a Democracy and are interested in checking out this learning and in acquiring more, some who know just enough to be curious, and others who will serendipitously become interested in its topic. The conduct of democracy is a daunting challenge. So was the writing of this book. The temptation from the beginning was to provide more detail than our commitment to a short book would allow. The result was that in each rewriting the goal was to cut. Necessarily, we chose to concentrate on major assumptions, fundamental ideas, and lessons learned. Consequently, this is not a how-to book. Perhaps this is a good thing, because there is no one best way to educate for democratic understanding and behavior. Indeed, we believe that the lack of a blueprint is a call to imagination and innovation—characteristics largely absent in school reform. The reader can readily find many suggestions for planning and acting in the publications cited.

This book attempts to capture the essence of an educational journey that has extended over several decades of the twentieth century and into the twenty-first. Three groups of people contributed to this journey in various ways. One group is composed of individuals who were, and still are in many cases, colleagues in one or more research and development initiatives in a series extending over several decades. When the book's three authors refer to what "we" did historically, this *we* encompasses all or part of this group, of which we, the authors, are members. Many of us have written about the activities in which we engaged, helping to build the knowledge base that is still accumulating. The present narrative draws heavily on the seventeen books, four dozen book chapters, and dozens of journal articles, technical reports, occasional papers, and other documents this "we" produced over the years. These works are listed by Kenneth Sirotnik in Appendix C of a companion volume, *Renewing Schools and Teacher Education*. The present book quotes extensively from these sources in its condensed portrayal of the concepts, principles, and understandings that evolved as the work progressed and ultimately generated the Agenda for Education in a Democracy.

The second group that has contributed significantly is less visible in the text. It is made up of a vast corps of philosophers, theologians, anthropologists, political scientists, psychologists, sociologists, and other wise women and men who have addressed the moral, political, economic, social, environmental, and other clusters of problems and issues that are embedded in what the authors and our colleagues call "the human conversation." From these clusters, both the collective "we" and the present writers have chosen to address democracy, education, and the critical relationship between the two. We use "the human conversation" as a metaphor for all of the associations in which the whole of humankind engages. Only a few of the people from this group are cited in this book, largely because so many of them have already been cited in the writings that are our primary sources. The wise people cited in these works wrote centuries or just a few years ago. Some of the most powerful ideas about democracy and education have been around for a long time. The reader is urged to remember that most of the sources cited also contain evidence of being significantly influenced in their thinking by this somewhat invisible array of contributors.

The third group of contributors to this book—the largest of the three groups—influenced our writing through their association with the initiatives described herein. These are the thousands of educators and others who have contributed time and effort to our work, usually over a period of years. A few from this group have written about their efforts. Many, however, have contributed to the testing of ideas—to the "proofing," as it were.

To all the members of these contributing groups we extend our deepest appreciation. In a way we serve in this writing as your prox-ies. To a degree this lets us off the hook of sole accountability. The obvious answer to this claim is that we are only interpreters. We did not ask any of you for specific instructions regarding the views you might have wished us to present. Had we done so, this book would not have been written, because doing justice to all of your diverse expectations would be impossible. We can only hope that we have represented you at an acceptable level of accuracy.

The three of us listed as the authors have had varying experi-ences with the subject matter over quite different periods. John I. Goodlad has been involved with all the educational initiatives dis-cussed, which date back to the late 1940s. Currently he is president of the nonprofit Institute for Educational Renewal, located in Seattle, close to the University of Washington. He is associated with its Center for Educational Renewal, which he and two colleagues created in 1985. Much of his writing that is relevant to our story is cited in the narrative.

Corinne Mantle-Bromley was involved with the Agenda for Education in a Democracy years before joining the IEI as its exec-utive vice president and the University of Washington as research professor in 2000. She brings to our ongoing work a rich back-ground of experience as a teacher in secondary schools and as a teacher and researcher in higher education. In her career at

Colorado State University before coming to Seattle, she piloted the role of hybrid educator in seeking to implement the Agenda through partnering the university and surrounding schools. From early on this partnership has been a member of the Colorado Partnership for Educational Renewal that in turn is a charter member of the National Network for Educational Renewal—a network of settings nationwide that are seeking to advance the Agenda as a guiding narrative for developing democratic character in the young.

Stephen John Goodlad is the most recent addition to the core staff of the work described here. He has taught at the University of Washington's Seattle and Bothell campuses and served part-time as a researcher at the IEI. To the Agenda for Education in a Democracy he has brought emphasis on the role that education must play in the often-ignored position of the environment in the well-being of democracy.

Seattle, Washington   John I. Goodlad
Summer 2003   Corinne Mantle-Bromley
                                                         Stephen John Goodlad

Chapter One

Schooling for Everyone

We have always had education, and it is always with us. Some of it is intentional; most of it is unintentional. In the history of humankind, schools are relatively new. The education they offer is intentional. Like all human creations, schools require our attention or they wither. Because the education that schools are to furnish is usually thought to be both important and not assured as part of the casual education routinely provided by the surrounding culture, presumably everyone in that culture should participate. In other words, the education made intentional through schooling should be universal.

The idea of education through *paideia*—by, in, and for the culture—has a long and noble tradition. It is represented in the initiation rites of cultures around the world. Anthropologist Alicja Iwańska describes a period of three to four weeks among Melanesians in the Bismarck Archipelago when adult males and females tell tales at night around the fire—tales that convey elements of the culture that are worthy of preservation. The narratives address etiquette, taboos, and customs, as well as punishments for those who break them.

In the southwestern United States, a part of the world closer at hand and more familiar to most of our readers than the Bismarck Archipelago, the Zuni Indians take collective responsibility for guiding any and all children's behavior. Around a communal bowl in the *kiva* (a usually round ceremonial structure that is partly underground) of the Hopi Indians, stories are told and retold in a process of spontaneous social education. "In the case of the Zuni

Indians, the self-appointed casual adults were the transmitters of the cultural heritage to children casually met; in the case of the Hopi, the elders of the community were the spontaneous educators; in the case of the [Melanesian] people of Lesu, the educators were the adult males and females. No one of those transmitters was even to the smallest degree a self-conscious specialist in educational planning."[1]

Drawing presumably from Greek and Roman tradition, *Webster's Third New International Dictionary* injects deliberate intent into the definition of *paideia*: "training of the physical and mental faculties in such a way as to produce a broad enlightened mature outlook harmoniously combined with maximum cultural development." In modern times, Mortimer Adler's definition has sharpened educational intent: "the equivalent of the Latin *humanitas* (from which 'the humanities'), signifying the general learning that should be the possession of all human beings."[2]

In *Webster's* and Adler's definitions are both the context that provides a necessary educational agenda for enculturating the members of the group, tribe, or community and the probable need for some kinds of mechanisms for ensuring universal attention to that agenda. Implicit in the well-being of the collective—not just of the individual—is an awareness that we, the people, however diverse we are, must live in a considerable degree of harmony with everybody and everybody's children, or else the group, the tribe, the community dissipates, disperses, or perishes. The evidence is in the history of humankind.

Education, Schooling, and Teaching

The idea that education through *paideia* provides a cultural transition from childhood to adulthood is very old. Embedded in this idea, apparently, is the operational concept of drawing the attention of the young to elements that are important to the culture's healthy continuation. Acquisition of the dispositions required for the retention of these elements necessitates repetition that in turn makes the necessary behavior routine. Twentieth-century psychologist B. F. Skinner built the contingencies to be repeatedly encountered by the inhabitants of his envisioned utopia as they walked the paths toward developing "a broad enlightened mature outlook harmoniously combined with maximum cultural development."[3] Ideally there would be much ongoing debate about the validity of the contingencies. Who would determine them? What values and virtues would be embedded in them? How should those contingencies decided upon be transmitted and by whom? What should be preserved?[4]

Herein lies a clutch of the most controversial issues surrounding yesterday's and today's conduct of schooling, the mechanism that, at an accelerating pace, came to be charged with taking the chance out of education through *paideia*. Some of the sense of adult responsibility for the enculturation of the young over a transitional period into adulthood has, over time, supported the development of educational institutions. As a consequence, schooling has helped to create and subsequently to expand childhood.[5]

The status of childhood and both parental and cultural expectations for the young have always been enmeshed in ambiguity. For how long and to what degree would the indiscretions of children be treated with educative intent before warranting the punishment befitting adult malfeasance? The schools created several hundred years ago for preparing European children for adulthood were to be instruments of strict discipline. Much of this concept of discipline was carried over into the early schools of the New World, where it is still alive today.

How long were the family and the community to await the aging of children into economic usefulness? Labor laws to protect children have been a long time in coming and are not yet universal. What should be the role of the schools in preparing the young for such usefulness? And should this role be differentiated to align with the hardened caste systems characterizing human existence? These alignments come in many forms, often subtle. The most obvious are differentiated schools, differentiated curricula within the same schools, and regularities—cultural norms—that differentiate access to education according to hierarchies of caste.

The most encompassing issue pertaining to an intentional period of education for the young through the institution of schooling is that of *mission*. Is the apparatus of schooling—purpose, conditions, modes of conduct—to be geared to a cultural ethos of child development or is it to be first and foremost an instrument dedicated to preparation for adulthood? Is it a system with children at its center or a system in which children and childhood are nuisances to the enterprise? If it is the latter, then schooling will have no moral compass.

The preceding discussion shows that *education* and *schooling* are not interchangeable words. Education is ubiquitous; it happens, everywhere. Operationally, on the one hand, it is a self-induced activity: nobody can give it to me, nobody can take it away. Schooling, on the other hand, is a planned, deliberate, intentional enterprise, part of the larger educational enterprise. Adults have something in mind for me to learn; they expect me to partake of that learning; they authorize teachers with the intent of seeing to it that I do learn. Of course, I don't have to. But contingencies are arranged on the assumption that they will make it easier for me to learn or, put another way, more difficult for me to escape the learning intended. Indeed, sometimes these contingencies make it dangerous for one not to learn. But they do not necessarily make the learning attractive and easier to acquire.

Contrary to popular belief, the concepts of education, schooling, and teaching are not necessarily inherently good. Further definition is necessary to make such a determination. They are, of course, all moral endeavors, but *moral*, too, is a morally neutral word. We learn to love or to hate, to give or to take, to kill or let live. The moral aspect—whether good or bad—is inseparable from culture, acquired through *paideia*, intentionally and unintentionally.

But a culture in which the good is deeply embedded cannot guarantee that everyone will come to possess the valued attributes. Creating a technology to explore outer space that includes the necessary human expertise is a piece of cake compared to forging the infrastructure necessary to accomplish a culture's most exalted moral educational mission—sustaining a wise citizenry. A culture that takes this mission lightly by delegating it solely to its schools is not wise. A culture that takes lightly the moral character of the whole of its teaching is doomed.

The reader may conclude that there is a contradiction in a moral mission that, on the one hand, places the nurturing of childhood first and, on the other, sees sustaining a wise citizenry as primary. Our answer is that the best preparation for the latter is the former. The roots of the self-transcendence characteristic of the mature adult are embedded in childhood. Teaching children about adulthood can excite their imaginations but probably will do little to help them with the contingencies of daily life. The best assurance of a broad, enlightened outlook combined with maximum cultural development in adulthood is its genesis in the culture of childhood. Children are engaged in learning every minute they are awake. It is the wise guiding of this learning that ensures a wise citizenry.

Part—a very important part—of this guidance is the teaching provided by schools. As a teacher of teachers said to a class of students preparing for such teaching, "Teaching is a moral endeavor and cannot help but be so." Shifting uneasily in his chair, a future teacher raised his hand and said, "As a teacher, I don't want to get involved in this moral stuff. It's just too controversial." He was not alone in his discomfort. Although people preparing to teach have little trouble with the concept that teaching has both good and bad consequences, few express the intention of becoming moral guidance counselors. Nonetheless, educational philosopher Gary Fenstermacher views teaching as inescapably having a moral dimension:

> What makes teaching a moral endeavor is that it is, quite centrally, human action undertaken in regard to other human beings. Thus, matters of what is fair, right, just, and virtuous are always present. Whenever a teacher asks a student to share something with another

student, decides between combatants in a schoolyard dispute, sets procedures for who will go first, second, third, and so on, or discusses the welfare of a student with another teacher, moral considerations are present. The teacher's conduct, at all times and in all ways, is a moral matter. For that reason alone, teaching is a profoundly moral activity.[6]

The pages that follow say much more about education writ large and about teaching in schools as a moral endeavor, as well as about the cultural sources that compete in the shaping of schools. The context envisioned as most desirable for this shaping is the work-in-progress called *democracy*. Democracy, wherever it is thought to exist, falls short of its own ideals. The authors agree with many thoughtful analysts, some of whom are cited in what follows, that education guided by these ideals is the driving force to the realization of these ideals and to their continuous renewal in the transforming world that is home to the whole of humankind.

Themes of This Book

There are two major themes in what follows and an array of subsidiary ones. Both major themes have been introduced in what precedes. First, there is in all cultures ongoing education for everyone. It is virtually as ubiquitous as the air we breathe. In modern, industrialized cultures, education provides a cacophony of teaching—some deliberate, some not—that challenges the interpreters, presents buzzing confusion, or creates a dulling impact for many.

Society commonly is reluctant to regard this as education. Only a couple of leaders in the television industry, during interviews conducted by a colleague, included education as one of the functions of this medium. All put forward entertaining and providing information; nearly all rejected educating. When the topic of education comes up, the thoughts of most people turn to schooling. As historian Lawrence Cremin once observed, it is folly to talk about educational improvement and excellence apart from the educational influence of families, peer groups, television and radio broadcasting (today we would add the Internet), the workplace, and more.[7]

Second, there is today in most countries schooling for some. We say "schooling for some" because schooling is an enterprise of the formal political structure. Those in power can and do determine how much schooling is available for whom and even who will learn what under what rules of inclusion and exclusion. Stratification in the regularities put in place often conforms to stratification in the cultural caste system.

Our argument is that the well-being of a *total* culture requires education for all, without exclusivity on the basis of caste: ethnicity, race, sex, heredity, religion, lifestyles and sexual preferences, wealth, assumed intelligence, physical disability, or whatever else humans are able to think up as bases for discrimination. Whatever the medium intended for educating, the provision of *total inclusion* is a moral imperative in a democracy and, it is essential to point out, a practical necessity for the health of all and for the continued renewal of a democratic culture.

The medium of deliberate, intended learning that we address in this book is schooling. We believe our theses (and the agenda we advance) to be appropriate and, we hope, appealing to other agencies committed to serving the public good. Health, welfare, social work, after-school enterprises, and other human services with educational dimensions come to mind. Hal Lawson, for example, has described the adaptation of our agenda by community collaboratives in the service of vulnerable children, youths, and families.[8]

The mission of society's intended learning, through whatever medium, is in large measure the product of its prevailing ethos. Authoritarian societies dictate mission; democratic societies ideally seek a working consensus. The latter is demanding and complex. As observant visitor Alexis de Tocqueville wrote more than a century and a half ago, our democracy is a daunting "apprenticeship of liberty."[9] Political scientist Benjamin Barber has said, "Public schools must be understood as public not simply because they serve the public, but because they establish us as a public"[10]—a democratic public. But he has also written, "Society undoes each workday what the school tries to do each school day."[11] To repeat Cremin's warning, it is folly to talk about educational excellence apart from the educational influence of the cacophony of teaching that is ongoing in the culture—thus our effort in what follows to address the interplay among the nation's ongoing experience with democracy, this ongoing educating, and the experiment in universal schooling with which the United States of America has long been engaged.

All societies want "educated" citizens, regardless of however any given society may chose to define the word *education*. Most modern societies, for example, want a literate population, able to read about and understand current events, laws, safety issues, and much more. Most want able-bodied, competent, cooperative workers. Most want their young to be enculturated into the social and political norms of the society. And in virtually all of these societies it is the schools that are largely responsible for doing whatever is necessary to try to meet these broad goals.

A democratic society is different from other kinds of societies in that while it looks to its schools to perform all of these essential functions, it also looks to its schools to create a very specific kind of citizen: a democratic citizen. A democracy can be successful only to the extent that its citizens are willing and able to assume the responsibilities of self-governance. Simply being literate is not enough. There is nothing democratic, for example, about being able to read the decrees of a dictator, or a racist, or a homophobe, or a fascist. So, while most modern societies may want their schools to produce "literate" people, a democracy demands a special kind of literacy that goes beyond merely comprehending words on a page or adding up columns of figures. It requires a literacy that includes such skills as critical inquiry; knowing how to ask questions and what kinds of questions need to be asked in a given circumstance; knowing how to evaluate the legitimacy and accuracy of an argument and the data that accompany it, to view issues from a variety of perspectives, and to evaluate the implications of a given text, read between the lines, and recognize and understand the unstated, the omitted, the subtext. In other words, literacy in a democracy is not only a special kind of literacy; it is also a more complex kind of literacy. And because of its uniqueness and its importance, teaching literacy in a democracy has a different kind of moral dimension than, say, teaching literacy under an authoritarian regime.

In the chapters ahead we explore in much greater detail the unique relationship between education and democracy, and the implications of that relationship for all of us in society. We also tell a story of sorts. It is the story of what has become the Agenda for Education in a Democracy. The Agenda guides a nationwide initiative that has evolved from several decades of inquiry into democracy, education, schooling, and cultural change. The Agenda seeks not only to reassert the centrality of preparation for democratic citizenship as the foremost mission of public schooling, but also to engage others—for example, politicians, journalists, parents, and sociologists—in ongoing collaborative processes of study, evaluation, and discussion aimed at furthering and improving this undertaking.

What follows in this chapter is a short history of the major activities that contributed to the substance of the Agenda, activities that involved many people. Chapter Two presents an abbreviated summary of the Agenda's mission, the conditions necessary to its conduct, and strategies for implementation. The Agenda is not a blueprint, nor is it a static plan for educational improvement. Like democracy itself, it is a work in progress.

The Agenda is designed to invite professional educators and all those community groups participating in or concerned about the vital role of education in our democracy to consider the Agenda's relevance to their interests and work. Our intent in Chapters Three through Seven is to bring the reader along through what was for us the formative work out of which the Agenda evolved, and then, in Chapter Eight, to return to its substance once again, highlighting major components, and to our experiences with its implementation. It would be interesting to know whether you come out where we did.

Beginnings: A Study of Schooling

There are many places we might choose to begin to tell the story of the Agenda for Education in a Democracy. We could, for example, go back to Aristotle and cobble together the theoretical foundations on which modern democracy rests. We could look at the struggles and debates of the framers of the U.S. Constitution. We could summon the literature describing early efforts to create a viable system of public education in this country and the many and diverse ideas that still surround and inform that ongoing process. And scattered among these places are many others—all of them compelling and worthy—where we might also begin to tell a story that has, it seems, many, many beginnings.

But just as there is no one beginning to our story, there is no one story either. Rather, the Agenda for Education in a Democracy emerges from many connecting and sometimes conflicting narratives. Like those narratives, the Agenda is an ongoing saga: continually evolving, responding to changes in the world around us, struggling to make itself better, more useful, more effective.

Nevertheless, with no beginning there can be no story. Kenneth Sirotnik wrestled with this problem when he and his colleagues assembled an evaluative report examining the work done by two educational agencies: the Center for Educational Renewal (CER) and the Institute for Educational Inquiry (IEI).[12] In this report, Sirotnik recalled a statement made by John Goodlad (one of the founders of both the CER and the IEI) in 1970: "Nothing short of a simultaneous reconstruction of preservice teacher education, in-service teacher education, and schooling itself will suffice if the [educational] change process is to be adequate."[13] What Goodlad then termed *reconstruction* would later evolve into the concept of *simultaneous renewal*, which we examine in much greater detail in the pages to come.

The genesis of the Agenda for Education in a Democracy became apparent in the mid-1980s when John Goodlad, Kenneth Sirotnik, and Roger Soder created the CER at the University of Washington. But this could not have occurred had the groundwork not been laid during the roughly fifteen years that preceded it. One critical component of what in retrospect might be regarded as a preparatory period was the Study of Educational Change and School Improvement (SECSI).

The SECSI was begun in the mid-1960s and centered on a collaborative effort involving eighteen elementary schools in eighteen different school districts working in partnership with the University of California at Los Angeles. This collaboration came to be known as the League of Cooperating Schools. The study itself was conducted by the Research Division of the Institute for Development in Educational Activities (IDEA) under the direction of John Goodlad.

From the SECSI there emerged several important concepts that would later inform much of the work of both the CER and the IEI. Among them were the following:

- Schools as both the center and unit of change
- The principal's crucial leadership role and the importance of developing a culture of individual and collective staff renewal
- An understanding of the dynamics of the change process that would come to be known as DDAE, or dialogue, decision making, action, and evaluation
- A better understanding of the ecology of educational change and the support structures essential to promoting it

Several of the League schools' principals would go on to serve as superintendents in other districts and to implement—with varying degrees of success—much of what they learned as a result of the study.

The impact of the SECSI findings and those of seminal studies conducted by many other researchers, reported in books and articles in the early to mid-1970s, was much less than it might have been had the nation not been engaged with challenging major social and political issues. By the end of the 1960s, education could no longer command the attention it had during the earlier part of the decade, when such federally funded reform efforts as the Elementary and Secondary Education Act of 1965 had received considerable popular support.

Wondering why so much effort had resulted in so little change, Frances Klein, John Goodlad, and several teachers in the laboratory school of the University of California Los Angeles (UCLA) began a series of inquiries that resulted in a pilot study that in turn launched a comprehensive, nationwide investigation of elementary and secondary schooling in the United States conducted by a team of researchers in the Research Division of IDEA and supported by several philanthropic foundations. The investigation was called A Study of Schooling. Its depth and scope have never been replicated. The researchers' findings were reported in numerous books and articles, among them *A Place Called School*.[14]

A Study of Schooling looked at the subjects being taught in our nation's classrooms; the methods used to teach them; the use of time by teachers and administrators; parental concerns and expectations; sources of satisfaction and dissatisfaction among teachers, students, and parents; the ongoing education of teachers; daily classroom rituals and routines; and so on. The resulting data indicated that the changes envisioned by political and educational leaders in the 1960s exceeded the systemic capabilities of elementary and secondary schooling at the time. The demands of teaching a variety of subjects with limited time and resources to classrooms of diverse students (in the case of secondary schools, to as many as 150 or more students per day) left little in the way of time, energy, or resources for teachers and administrators to deal with the vast complexities of systemic change. "It was and is bizarre to think," Sirotnik has said, "that periodic faculty meetings in the late afternoon can accomplish anything other than changes (mostly cosmetic) in daily routines."[15]

The findings of A Study of Schooling offered an interesting counterpoint to the 1983 report *A Nation at Risk: The Imperative for Educational Reform*, which emphasized our nation's economic interests and sought to change many of the practices of schooling. The report stated the following:

> Our nation is at risk. Our once unchallenged preeminence in commerce, industry, science, and technological innovation is being overtaken by competitors throughout the world. . . . What was unimaginable a generation ago has begun to occur—others are matching and surpassing our educational attainments.
>
> If an unfriendly foreign power had attempted to impose on America the mediocre educational performance that exists today, we might well have viewed it as an act of war. As it stands, we have allowed this to happen to ourselves. We have even squandered the gains in student achievement made in the wake of the Sputnik challenge. Moreover, we have dismantled essential support systems which helped make those gains possible. We have, in effect, been committing an act of unthinking, unilateral educational disarmament.[16]

The report went on to propose that schools be restructured to meet the demands of a newly emerging global economy. The central mission and basic tenets in *A Nation at Risk* were to remain a focal point for many educators for years to come. The report itself, and many that would follow, largely ignored the findings of A Study of Schooling, as well as of two other major studies of secondary education, one by Ernest Boyer in 1983 and another by Theodore Sizer in 1984.

The Education of Educators

In 1979, John Goodlad, Kenneth Sirotnik, and Paul Heckman created the Laboratory in School and Community Education (LSCE) at UCLA. A major initiative of the LSCE was the development of a closely knit school-university partnership that served as a generating model for more ambitious programs in subsequent years. Throughout the 1980s, the LSCE launched a number of other initiatives.

One was the Southern California School-University Partnership, which consisted of more than a dozen school districts, five county school offices, two community colleges, and UCLA. The collaboration was based primarily on the idea that there existed "a critical mass of individuals interested in collaborating with persons of like concern and willing to tackle together the educational problems of their time—and even to assume some personal and professional risk in the process."[17]

The Southern California School-University Partnership improved on the stratagem of the League of Cooperating Schools by bringing in school superintendents as major players (they had largely been relegated to the role of approving observers in previous undertakings) as well as by vastly expanding the role of the university in helping to bring about change. This work caught the attention of the college of education at Brigham Young University (BYU). In the autumn of 1983, John Goodlad was invited to work with that institution and its five surrounding school districts in an effort to simultaneously rethink the mission of the college of education at BYU while forging strategic partnerships with these districts. This work marks the beginning of what would later become a major initiative to encourage and support the development of school-university partnerships nationwide.

Goodlad relocated to the University of Washington in 1984. His longtime friend and colleague Kenneth Sirotnik moved to the University of Washington in 1985. Together they teamed up with a new colleague, Roger Soder, and the three of them created the CER there in 1985.

Initially, the CER had two primary purposes. First, building on earlier research, it was to conduct a new study to examine how educators were being prepared for their professions. Second, it was to help build, support, and sustain a nationwide network of school-university partnerships engaged in the work of improving the conditions of schooling based on all that had been learned in the research prior to and concurrent with its founding.

This initiative was somewhat unique in that it would make a determined effort to combine both inquiry and practice. A primary target for research would be teacher education. Whereas A Study of Schooling had focused on the conditions and practices of K–12 schooling, the institutions—colleges and universities—that actually prepare educators for our nation's schools had received relatively little scrutiny.

Over the course of the latter half of the 1980s, Goodlad, Sirotnik, and Soder went to work on what would come to be called the Study of the Education of Educators (SEE). This study inquired into programs around the country that prepared teachers, administrators, and special educators. It looked at the interrelationships among the K–12 schools themselves and the university schools of education and departments of arts and sciences that served to help prepare our nation's teachers. Like those of its predecessors, the findings of the SEE research were reported in numerous books, articles, and technical reports. Of particular note, the research confirmed that Goodlad and his colleagues had been correct in their earlier assessments that the idea of simultaneous renewal was not only valid as an approach to educational change but perhaps also essential if such change was to be significant and lasting.

Along with the idea of simultaneous renewal was born the idea of the *center of pedagogy*. As envisioned, a center of pedagogy is both a physical entity and a conceptual ideal. Conceptually, a center of pedagogy combines the various—and usually scattered—elements of teacher education "and embeds them in reflective attention to the art and science of teaching." A center of pedagogy is different from what one might call a center of teacher education in that the latter would probably "embrace only what the name implies—the conduct of teacher education programs devoid of or apart from inquiry into pedagogy. The common neglect of such inquiry has contributed to the low status of teacher education and, to a considerable degree, of teaching itself."[18]

In *Educational Renewal,* Goodlad elaborates further on the idea of a center of pedagogy:

> The term *center of pedagogy* connotes for me an inquiring setting for the education of educators that embraces schools and universities.
>
> Unfortunately, teacher education has come to be associated only with training and the mechanistic ways we teach dogs, horses, and humans to perform certain routinized tasks. This is largely because we have reduced our view of education to such. But teaching in the schools *must not* be perceived this way. . . .
>
> How humans learn and how they can best be taught are subjects of great importance and profound complexity. For teacher education programs not to be connected with ongoing inquiry into these domains is to guarantee their mediocrity and inadequacy. The best assurance for this connection is for teacher education to be conducted in centers of inquiry focused on this learning and teaching—that is, in centers of pedagogy where the art and science of teaching are brought to bear on the education of educators and where the *whole* is the subject of continuous inquiry.[19]

While the staff of the CER was conducting its inquiry into the education of educators, a more ambitious effort was beginning to take shape: an effort that would attempt to translate theory into practice. That effort ultimately centered on the founding of the National Network for Educational Renewal (NNER), a nation-wide coalition of school-university partnerships working to improve what goes on in schools and classrooms. The collaborating school districts and universities in each NNER partnership agreed to work together to address three primary goals:

1. To promote exemplary performance by universities in their role of educating educators
2. To promote exemplary performance by schools in their role of educating the nation's young people

3. To promote constructive collaboration between schools (and their districts) and universities in ensuring exemplary performance of overlapping mutual self-interests, especially the simultaneous renewal of schools and the education of workers for them.[20]

As work on the development of the NNER and the CER continued, the need to address the "political" and "content" issues of schooling became increasingly apparent. It was recognized that schooling must have a shared, agreed-upon purpose to be relevant and effective. That purpose found its voice in what would become known as the Agenda for Education in a Democracy.

Chapter Two

Agenda for Education in a Democracy

The Agenda for Education in a Democracy grew out of "a set of strong beliefs and assumptions about the nature of educational and organizational change and about the purposes of public education in a democracy," Kenneth Sirotnik has explained.

> Beliefs guiding educational and organizational change included collaborative leadership, empowerment of participants, critical inquiry and reflective practice, goals arising out of activity rather than goals driving activity, formative evaluation, and so on. Likewise, guiding assumptions about the purposes and structure of public education in a democracy included such notions as preparing well educated, creative, and thoughtful citizens able to participate actively and critically in our democracy, ensuring equal access to the best educational practices for all students, and creating caring and socially just environments that model how equity and excellence can go hand in hand.[1]

For some people, schools were and often still are thought of as simply places where youngsters go to learn how to read, write, and do arithmetic. If schools are thought to have a broader social mandate, that mandate is usually to prepare the young for entry into the workforce. But generally speaking, "schools suffer from a lack of a clearly articulated mandate and so are particularly susceptible to fads and fashions. These in turn become matters for legislative attention, which too often produces just more emergency splints, each holding in place a joint thought to be malfunctioning."[2]

The history of schooling in America suggests that schools have a more important role to play than is often recognized. The "school is the only institution in our nation specifically charged with enculturating the young into a social and political democracy," Goodlad points out. "Schools, through their teachers, must introduce our young people to the ideas inherent in our political democracy and the ideals from which they are derived."[3] As A Study of Schooling revealed, this mission enjoys rather widespread support among parents, teachers, and students.

The beliefs and assumptions that had begun to emerge from the SEE, as well as changes in schooling that were being reported in professional journals and in the media, began to give rise to a more formalized set of ideas about the conditions and practices necessary for the education of educators. These ideas—they would come to be called *postulates* and there were roughly twenty of them—would in turn fuel the ongoing SEE inquiry.

The data highlighted five specific areas deserving of attention:

1. The need for structural conditions supportive of institutional leadership and commitment, reward systems for faculty, and autonomy and fiscal security for the programs offered

2. Faculty responsibilities, qualifications, and accountability

3. The responsibilities of program with respect to developing future educators committed to both equity and excellence

4. Preparing students to deal with the realities of schooling, constructive criticism, the development of student cohorts, and the cultivating of supportive and evaluative links with graduates

5. Regulatory and policy conditions; issues of licensing, certification, and accreditation; and the need to prevent "backdoor" entry into the profession that would result in unprepared and unqualified teachers and administrators

Once postulates had been formulated, the specific questions that would drive the SEE study were self-evident.[4]

Prior to conducting the study, one state was selected in each of the eight major census regions of the country. In each of these states, from two to six institutions were chosen for careful study. In all, twenty-nine settings comprising each type of teacher-preparing college or university in the United States, some public, some private, were chosen.

The SEE data offered little in the way of surprise or gratification. Not a single program was found to be exemplary in any of the five areas just listed, let alone all of them. There were some hopeful signs, however. For instance, one program might have a carefully thought-out philosophy undergirding it. Another might offer a rather well-conceived and developed series of courses. Another might excel in the area of educational research. Still, it was evident that there was much room for improvement, including the development of partnerships among colleges of education, arts and science departments, and schools—relationships that were commonly absent in the education of educators.

"Many of the programs visited, in fact, were rather dismally far from being exemplary in any respect," Sirotnik recalled. "It was almost as if they were operating under a set of principles equal to the negations of the . . . postulates."[5] It was learned, for example, that faculty members were often frustrated by intrusive and restrictive policies and requirements. Some believed that simply being familiar with a particular subject matter qualified them to teach it. Most lacked a clear sense of mission or a philosophical grounding or framework, or even a sense that there might be moral responsibilities inherent in the teaching profession.

In summarizing the SEE findings in 1990, it was evident, wrote one researcher, that "there is a great deal of blame to spread around; once again, there is little to be gained in doing so. The legacies from yesterday contribute their share of problems, as does the context of higher education in which teacher education is lodged."[6] Sirotnik adds, "Unlike the education-bashing writers who always look for easy targets to trash, our goal was to report it as we saw it, with the intent of finding constructive ways to talk about improving teacher education. And we had no intention of letting anyone off the hook, including ourselves, as faculty and researchers in a college of education at a research university."[7]

The SEE suggested that educators would benefit by adopting the conditions and courses of action indicated by the postulates that had come to drive the study. But this idea would not be easy to implement. For one thing, the postulates were not blueprints for change. They were conceptual. Each contained ideas and propositions, but not recipes or directions for action. There were no clear roadmaps to say "this is how we get there."

Instead, the propositions referred to as postulates were developed with the assumption that those involved in implementing them would be competent professionals with abilities and ideas that would prove valuable if they were given the chance to make use of them. A premium was placed on collaboration among educators working to achieve goals that they themselves articulated. Sirotnik summed it up this way: "The people on the frontlines were going to have to invent and reinvent their own missions and practices, given their own state, community, and institutional contexts."[8]

At a glance, the postulates *looked* simple and even, to a degree, seemed obvious, but this was to prove deceptive. As implementation got under way, it became clear that to be useful the postulates would first need to undergo an "unpacking" process. As A Study of Schooling had demonstrated years earlier, change is all but impossible if the system in place is not designed to be receptive to new ideas. The coalition of school-university partnerships named the National Network for Educational Renewal (NNER), officially launched in 1986, proved to be crucial in learning just how to translate theory into practice.

A core belief held by those in the NNER was that good schools require good teachers and good teacher preparation programs require good schools. This belief meant that school-university partnerships would play a central role in the work and structure of the NNER. It also brought to the fore the notion of simultaneous renewal. In other words, if you really wanted to improve schools, you had to get everyone involved in the process to work together as a team with a shared mission. School-university partnerships provided the structure, simultaneous renewal provided the process, and the postulates articulated the conditions necessary to advance the mission of the Agenda for Education in Democracy.

National Network for Educational Renewal

Initially, the NNER consisted of ten school-university partnerships in ten states. These usually comprised a school or college of education in a research university teamed with several school districts and selected schools within those districts. The key theoretical concept behind the partnerships was to develop a positive symbiotic relationship that would enable the collaborators to benefit mutually from their interactions while avoiding the pitfalls of a negative symbiosis wherein partners become dependents. To this end, certain criteria were outlined and participants screened to try to ensure they would meet those criteria.

The purposes of the partnerships were three:

1. To improve the performance of universities as institutions responsible for educating our nation's teachers. This included not only bettering teacher education programs, but making better use of university research as well.
2. To improve the performance of schools and of the school districts that provide crucial support to the mission of public education.
3. To improve the collaborative relationships among schools, districts, and universities so that all would be able to work together more effectively, to the mutual benefit of everyone involved.

The agenda that grounded these early NNER school-university partnerships comprised a list of ideals that would address a particular set of issues that seemed at times almost impossibly intractable. As John Goodlad once explained, "One begins with such problems because they are there; they won't go away. But one does not pursue for long either the problems of the 1960s or those of the 1980s without coming to the realization that they are manifestations of educational and, indeed, sociopolitical issues of long standing. What appears to be quite contemporary is found to have a long lineage."[9]

From what was learned, elements critical to the improvement of schools include the creation of exemplary teacher education programs that make effective use of what is known about how schools best function; the development of curricula that reflect the needs of students and the assurance of equal access for all students to these curricula; the restructuring of schools to improve the continuity of students' programs, to deal better with problems of alienation and dropping out, and to enable teachers to make better use of available resources; and the cultivation of an ongoing, informed dialogue at the community level about what education is, why it is important, and what it means to the welfare of individuals and of society as a whole.

Structurally, the partnerships were organized to facilitate widespread understanding and cooperation among members while minimizing bureaucratic interference and red tape. These structures included arrangements for sharing ideas, information, and resources; ways of redirecting existing funds as well as securing external funding for particular projects and innovations; ways of documenting, analyzing, and communicating successes and failures within the network; and a formal commitment to participate for a period of at least five years.

The NNER came to provide, in effect, an intricate web of connections among the different partnerships. This web worked to facilitate the exchange of ideas, practices, information, and even personnel among the participants. As a result, the NNER was intentionally structured to provide comprehensive access to a growing body of data and analysis. Study groups were organized to seek solutions to common problems. Periodic meetings and conferences were scheduled, newsletters were published, and consultants were brought in where specific situations warranted particular expertise.

At the heart of the NNER was an effort to draw attention to the unique role of education in a democratic society and the need to foster sound educational policies and practices that would not only support the broad purposes of democratic schooling but would also make possible the ongoing process of renewal.

As the Center for Educational Renewal (CER) and the National Network for Educational Renewal (NNER) continued to develop in the early 1990s, much work was devoted to achieving three primary objectives. First, despite the numerous books, reports, and articles published in preceding years, it was apparent that educators needed and wanted more specific ideas and more detailed discussions than had been presented up to that time. A major objective would be to further refine and elaborate on this new vision of schooling.

A second objective arose from the feeling that while good and useful work had been done, much remained to be done to make the simultaneous renewal of schools and the education of educators a concrete reality. The solution seemed to be to develop clusters of pilot settings that could effectively serve as models for implementing the Agenda. This meant, in other words, "the coming together of educators from the schools and the colleges and universities in equal partnerships to put real meat on the bones of the Agenda and to give it shape, character, and viability in the context of their own conditions and circumstances."[10] As one staffer put it, "It was time to fish or cut bait."

The third objective that arose at that time proved too ambitious and was eventually abandoned. This objective was the result of pressures that were being brought to bear by the Education Commission of the States and the American Association of Colleges of Teacher Education (AACTE) on the CER to scale up its operations in collaboration with these two organizations. As envisioned, this "ramping up" would require a national effort to implement the recommendations of the Agenda in at least one school-university collaborative in all fifty states by 1995.

It was realized that increasing the size of the NNER would present problems of scale in their own right. A better approach, it seemed, would be to try to demonstrate genuine, lasting success in a few key areas. If this could be done, it was believed, then other partnerships would want to develop similar models. We would scale up at a manageable pace.

Although it was eventually abandoned, this third objective did facilitate important, ongoing policy work at both the institutional and the state levels. It also laid the groundwork for a valuable and ongoing collaboration among the CER, the NNER, the AACTE, and the Education Commission of the States.

The programs, models, experiences, experiments, studies, and ideas that preceded and fueled the Agenda involved the concerted efforts of many talented and dedicated individuals, but a comprehensive understanding of the Agenda and its implications for schooling and for the education of educators remained the privileged view of a minority. For the Agenda to be successful, it would be essential for everyone involved to gain this more comprehensive perspective.

The postulates that articulated the conditions and practices necessary for the education of educators and that drove the Study of the Education of Educators received mixed responses from university settings. Kenneth Sirotnik recalled:

> Some thought that the postulates were an exercise in stating the obvious, some thought they were impossible to realize, and some thought they were too vague and did not spell out the details of what was actually necessary to accomplish whatever was being suggested. Some understood quite well what was being suggested and assured us they were already doing it all. Others, who also claimed to understand the ideas, indicated the postulates were off base or misdirected or even unnecessary. Ironically, no one disputed the findings of our study![11]

Given that the major thrust of the work being done by the CER in the 1990s was to promote and support efforts to implement the renewal agenda of the NNER, clearly a major effort would have to be undertaken to try to unpack the postulates in such a way that the ideas and implications they contained were clear and accessible to all concerned. "It was a tricky business," Sirotnik explained; "we knew full well that detailed blueprints and exhortations to follow them never work. Surely the postmortems of major educational change efforts, if they have told us anything, have said that." The idea was "to get specific enough to leave no question of the commitments involved and yet leave room enough for the kind of creative interpretations and adaptations almost sure to be necessary in any particular circumstance."[12]

More than that, it would be necessary to find ways to reach out to skeptics and to persuade them of the merits of the Agenda. Language had to be developed to talk to those who saw the postulates as obvious or vague or impossible or even downright unnecessary. Two books, *The Moral Dimensions of Teaching* and *Teachers for Our Nation's Schools*, had done much to communicate the arguments supporting the Agenda. But clearly more was needed. There had to be a way to get others to examine their own programs and beliefs seriously and constructively. The CER's collaborations with the AACTE and the Education Commission of the States would prove to be crucial assets.

Building on the information and recommendations that resulted from the Study of the Education of Educators, a series of statewide conversations were arranged to coincide with the release of the SEE reports. These conversations, which occurred in twenty-five states, brought together representatives from schools, colleges, and universities as well as from the business community, state legislatures, and the public at large to examine in detail the moral, political, and educational implications of the Agenda. From these conversations emerged what would become formally known as the Agenda for Education in a Democracy.

The Four-Part Mission of Schooling

In the context of much that was going on in schools and teacher education programs at the time, the Agenda presented a new and very different vision of schooling. In *Educational Renewal: Better Teachers, Better Schools*, John I. Goodlad wrote:

> The most critically important omission [in teacher education] is a vision that encompasses a good and just society, the centrality of education to the renewal of that society, the role of schools in bringing this education equitably to all, and the kind of preparation teachers require for their stewardship of the nation's schools. This is the vision that provides the moral grounding of the teacher education mission and gives direction to those teachers of teachers responsible for designing coherent programs for the education of educators.[13]

Schools are not often thought of or spoken of as institutions having moral imperatives. But the skills, dispositions, and habits of intellect necessary for democratic citizenship have to be developed somewhere. People are not born with them. This places a considerable burden on the shoulders of teachers, who are responsible to the children they teach as well as to their parents and to society as a whole. The moral dimensions of teaching are inescapable. When a teacher begins to teach, a whole array of moral choices and decisions inescapably comes into play. What is omitted from a curriculum can be just as consequential as what is included. How information is presented can have a tremendous effect on how it is received. Teaching cannot help but be informed by values and guided by normative principles.[14]

The initial idea for this work was to present the moral components of teaching as one leg of a four-legged stool on which the teaching profession rests. Together the four legs would represent the four fundamental parts of the mission of schooling. But we soon realized

> that normative considerations are part of each leg and do not constitute a discrete entity. They pervade the whole, becoming moral

imperatives for teaching, a profession of teaching, and teacher education. These moral imperatives arise out of the school's responsibility for enculturating the young, the necessity for and challenge of providing access to knowledge for all students, the unique relationship between the teacher and the taught in the context of compulsory schooling, and the role of teachers in renewing school settings.[15]

The school's responsibility for enculturating the young into America's social and political culture was recognized early in our nation's history, when schools began to receive financial support from taxpayers. With the founding of the republic, the idea of enculturation became more pronounced and the rhetoric of the day emphasized the role that schools were to play in shaping responsible young adults as citizens, as parents, and as workers.[16]

The history of schooling very much mirrors that of our society as a whole. Like the society in which our schools are embedded, inequality and injustice have proven extremely difficult to overcome. For educators this suggests that "the general education of all schoolteachers must provide them with critical perspectives (historical, philosophical, and sociological) on the nature of democratic societies, with particular reference to their own political democracy. This is not now ensured by passage through an undergraduate curriculum." Moreover, teachers "need to acquire both an understanding of the critical role of schools in enculturating the young and a sense of moral justice regarding the right of all to the necessary education." This aspect of the mission of schooling should be nonnegotiable: "Our society simply cannot afford teachers who fail to understand and assume the moral burden that goes with developing humane individuals within the context of a political democracy. Teacher-preparing institutions share the moral burden."[17] In short, one part of the four-part mission of schooling as articulated by the proponents of the Agenda for Education in a Democracy can be succinctly stated as *enculturating the young into a social and political democracy*.

Providing access to knowledge for all children and youths is a second component of the four-part mission of schooling. One of the most commonly expressed goals for schooling is to promote the development and use of the intellect through encounters with various bodies of knowledge. Too often, though, what is understood to be "knowledge" amounts to little more than inert bits and pieces that, taken together, amount to little more than the leftovers or refuse of what could be called the *human conversation*. Mere exposure to this refuse is not the same as genuine, substantive participation in the conversation itself. It is precisely such participation, such active engagement, that is too often lacking as schools strive to provide access only to selected fragments. Participation in the human conversation and access to all the varied knowledge that goes with it are important because they are what develops a person's intellectual and social skills and abilities and what best prepares that person to interpret the human experience. Such skills and abilities can in turn do much to increase prospects for living a rich, engaged, and vital life.

Systemic failures in this area have been predictable. Opportunities to gain access to the most generally useful knowledge have traditionally been poorly distributed within and among most schools. Poor and minority youngsters are those most frequently disenfranchised. From a moral perspective, this is simply wrong regardless of the arguments that may be made concerning teachable classes, teachers' comfort, parents' preferences, and achievement levels. What this suggests is that future teachers must not be allowed to remain ignorant or unconcerned about such matters, and their professional preparation must strive to ensure a necessary loss of innocence.[18]

A third part of the mission concerns the relationship between the teacher and the taught and is generally referred to in the Agenda as *practicing pedagogical nurturing* with respect to *the art and science of teaching*. Because our society requires that children attend school (or some reasonable equivalent), a quite special and unique burden is placed on the teacher. The teacher-student relationship in public schools takes on a moral dimension that is fundamentally different from, for example, that which exists for private schools.

The problems that arise as a result of this relationship are many. Foremost among them is the simple fact that students do not freely choose to be in school. Moreover, it is often the case that

> they see little there as utilitarian in their lives; the connections between classes or courses and personal betterment of some kind are remote. Intrinsic motivation, so lauded in psychological literature, is largely missing. Our research has shown that the likelihood of intrinsic motivation being present for athletics, vocational subjects, and the arts is greater than for history, algebra, and mathematics. The first three rank high in liking and interest among many secondary school students, but it is English, mathematics, science, and social studies that are most valued in schools and required for admission to college. Students' motivation for these subjects is closely tied to their motivation for more school. This kind of motivation, in turn, is tied to family background and economic status and is unevenly distributed in the culture.[19]

The practical and moral implications of compulsory schooling—and the impact they have on the judgments that teachers are routinely called on to make—are complex. For example, does the child who was absent for illness have a greater right to make up time with a teacher than does the child whose parents simply kept him or her out? Time to learn is an exceedingly important factor in students' accomplishments, but how much additional time for Marie is warranted? Is it all right to deny Tom his interest in drawing when he does not finish his arithmetic? To further complicate matters, the "moral crunch for many decisions made by people outside of schools finally comes down to teachers in schools." In other words, we "want our teachers to be sensitive and caring, but the more they are, the greater [will be] the decision-making dilemmas in which they find themselves. The more limited our vision of what teaching in schools is and what it requires of teachers, their preparation, and their support, the more we shortchange them and ourselves."[20]

A fourth part of the mission aims at *ensuring responsible stewardship of the schools*. The idea is this: "If schools are to become the responsive, renewing institutions that they must, the teachers in them must be purposefully engaged in the renewal process. It does not matter whether a good deal of the impetus and many of the ideas for reform come from outside, so long as what comes into the school is seen as reasonable and useful by those engaged on the inside." Yet there would be

> irresponsibility in significantly expanding teachers' authority without [also] educating them to use it well. Using it well requires both knowledge and moral sensitivity. These are acquired, in large part, through critical, disciplined socialization into the full array of expectations and responsibilities a democratic society requires of its teachers. This is unlikely to occur if teaching in schools is seen to require only the generic skills common to all teaching. Nor is it likely to occur if passage through a general undergraduate curriculum and mentoring with an experienced teacher are to be the route to teaching, as is so frequently recommended. Nor is this disciplined socialization commonly occurring in teacher education programs as now conducted.[21]

Education and Schooling

The central question that the four-part mission of schooling attempts to address is, What are schools for? If the only purpose of schools is simply to teach youngsters to read, write, and do arithmetic, then the

> job can be done inexpensively and efficiently through computer-based skill centers in the local shopping mall. "Park your kid in the spelling lab and shop," blinks the new sign, twenty-four hours a day. A teaching profession built on generic principles of teaching is an expensive hoax.

But if the answer to the question of what schools are for is more complex—is seen to encompass such things as responsibility for critical enculturation into a political democracy, the cultivation (with the family) of character and decency, and preparation for full participation in the human conversation—then teachers (carefully selected teachers, themselves well educated, who understand the layers of contextual complexity and who have engaged in reflection and dialogue on the moral issues involved) become necessary. Such teachers and their calling warrant the designation "professional." They must be both liberally and professionally educated.[22]

Schools do not exist in vacuums. They are embedded in a vast and complex social, political, and economic surround. They interact with that surround continuously. Schools affect their cultural context, and their context in turn affects them. It is not possible to have good, healthy, democratic schools in an environment that is hostile to such qualities. We often ask, in various ways, if our schools are safe for society, if they are protecting our youth and other citizens, if they are championing "the right" values, if they are exercising adequate discipline to ensure cooperation and orderliness, and so on. Less often, however, do we ask if society is safe for our schools; if our society demonstrates by example the qualities we hope our schools will instill in the young; if our social, political, and economic policies and behaviors reflect the values we want our schools to champion; if the neighborhoods children walk through to get to school are safe, clean, healthy places for children to be; if the adult world exercises the levels of cooperation and orderliness that many feel are so essential to foster in the young.

"There is a contextual surround that invariably shapes the educational process," Goodlad explains. "The political context is critical. The shaping that takes place in a fascist or communist régime is quite different from that in a democracy. The social context is equally, or perhaps even more, critical. People who live by sword and gun raise their children by very different beliefs than do people who value negotiation as the proper way to resolve disagreements."[23]

As stated earlier, *schooling* and *education* are not interchangeable words. To the extent that education works to develop the individual within a particular cultural context, it is essentially the same the world over. But with respect to the nature of the interaction that takes place between an individual and a particular cultural surround, education may—and often does—vary widely. The qualities of schools and what they have to offer do not and cannot exist independently of their cultural surround.

Schooling can be useful in its achievement of official public purpose, yet still fail to provide a good *education* in a context dominated by repression and punishment. This leads one to conclude that "the proper context for education is a politically and socially democratic one. Not a half-formed democracy of slogans and rituals but a work in progress that . . . [is] continuously self-conscious about the degree to which it is safe for education in its fostering of decency, civility, justice, freedom, and caring. Such fostering is not the responsibility nor within the capability of schools alone."[24]

What is meant by "a politically and socially democratic" context? How do we differentiate between a legitimately democratic context and "a half-formed democracy of slogans and rituals"? To answer these questions and so to understand and appreciate fully the Agenda for Education in a Democracy, some understanding of our nation's history, the nature of democracies, and the forces that help shape and define them is necessary. We take up these issues in the next chapter.

Chapter Three

The Context of Schooling
in a Democracy

"Public schools are not merely schools *for* the public," political scientist Benjamin Barber once wrote, "but schools of publicness: institutions where we learn what it means to *be* a public and start down the road toward common national and civic identity. They are the forges of our citizenship and the bedrock of our democracy."[1]

Many people assume that the United States has a democratic system of governance, that this system was established early on in our nation's history by the framers of the U.S. Constitution, that it is so thoroughly embedded in our collective psyche that it is invulnerable to external threats, that it is an inheritance handed down from one generation to the next, and that all we have to do to maintain it is occasionally to vote.

But democracy is a daunting work in progress that should never be taken for granted. There is nothing that says it will exist fifty years from now or, for that matter, until next week. There is nothing that guarantees that our judges and politicians will respect the rule of law or the principles of the Constitution. There is nothing that guarantees that our leaders will serve the best interests of the American people or will share the fear of political tyranny that fired the hearts and minds of the nation's founders. The dictatorships of both Adolf Hitler and Benito Mussolini were spawned in democracies. As history demonstrates, democracies often collapse and can do so quite easily unless systems are in place to ensure the vigilance and active participation of a healthy and committed citizenry. Of paramount importance to this undertaking is public education. For this reason, a crucial component of the Agenda for Education in a Democracy centers on the need to educate the American public about schools and the roles they must play in both promoting and sustaining our democracy.

Roger Soder has often addressed the relationship between schooling and democracy in his speeches. In discussing the reasons and need for the Agenda, Soder asks audiences if they want to live in a democracy. They respond with a nod. Soder then asks if they agree that citizens in a democracy have to possess skills and dispositions that are different from those of citizens not living in democracies. The answer usually requires a moment's thought, but again there is a nodding of heads. Where and how are such skills and dispositions to be acquired, Soder asks.

Soder's point is a simple and, one might think, obvious one, but as audience after audience has discovered, few of us really think much about what it means to live in a democracy or what is needed to sustain one. Most of us understand that schools are supposed to teach youngsters to read, write, and figure. Most of us assume that schools will do something to prepare the young to enter the workforce. We also assume that schools will make youngsters computer literate. But little thought is given to educating for citizenship in a social and political democracy, to developing the character, competence, and skills necessary for such citizenship. Yet democracies never *just happen*. They have to be created, nurtured, promoted, and protected, or they perish. In other words, democracy places a unique responsibility on the shoulders of both educators and the public they serve. It is not a responsibility assigned by administrators or political leaders. It is a moral responsibility, a responsibility that should be assumed by all concerned because it is unconscionable not to assume it.

The Relationship Between Public Schooling and Democracy

It is nice to think that all youngsters have parents and that all parents have the time, patience, knowledge, skills, abilities, and will to educate their children in the democratic arts. There are some for whom this is the case. But it is not the case for most of us. That is why for an education in democracy to be effective and meaningful, it must be made available to all members of the society. "Public schooling and the public weal," Barber reminds us, "are intimately bound together."[2]

In *Democracy, Education, and the Schools*, historian Robert B. Westbrook has this to say about the connection between democracy and schools:

> The relationship between public schooling and democracy is a conceptually tight one. Schools have become one of the principle institutions by which modern states reproduce themselves, and insofar as those states are democratic, they will make use of schools to prepare children for democratic citizenship. The very notion of democratic "public" education reflects this fact: democratic public schools are ostensibly not only schools supported by public finance but schools that educate every student for the responsibilities and benefits of participating in public life. One reasonable measure of the strengths and prospects of a democracy is the degree to which its public schools successfully devote themselves to this task.[3]

Implicit in Westbrook's statement is the concern that a nation that fails to take seriously the need to prepare its young for democratic citizenship is a nation that places its democracy in serious jeopardy. The framers of the Constitution understood this and also recognized the role of education in a democratic society. Thomas Jefferson was one of the most outspoken and articulate on the subject. While the Constitution declared that all men are "born free," Jefferson, Barber reminds us, "knew well enough that liberty is acquired and that citizens are educated to a responsibility that comes to no man or woman naturally. Without citizens, democracy is a hollow shell. Without public schools, there can be no citizens."[4]

Characteristics of a Democratic People

Citizens in a democratic society must be prepared to assume those responsibilities commensurate with any group or population committed to self-governance. This is different from a citizenry that is governed by a privileged elite with essentially dictatorial powers, no matter how benevolent. Therefore a good deal more is required of democracy's citizens than merely voting come election day. As Julie Underwood explains,

> The founders of the United States believed that the success of American democracy depended on the development of an educated citizenry who would vote wisely, protect its own rights and freedoms, rout out political corruption, and keep the nation secure from internal and external threats to democracy. Strong character and moral virtue were considered an essential part of good citizenship. Early leaders generally endorsed Thomas Jefferson's statement that "a people who mean to be their own Governors must arm themselves with the power which knowledge gives."[5] More than any others, Jefferson's words express the "common school" philosophy that swept the nation in its development.[6]

There is a difference between voting and voting wisely, just as there is a difference between simply having an opinion and having what we might call an *informed* opinion. The people cited in this book have opinions about what education is and about what it ought to be, as do the book's authors. These opinions are generally based on years of research, application, discussion, evaluation, and reflection. They are, in other words, not just opinions but *informed* opinions: opinions based on more than "feelings" or vague perceptions or hearsay. The authors of this book might, for example, have opinions about how best to repair jet aircraft engines, but these would not be *informed* opinions. No matter how well intentioned or how persuasively and passionately these opinions are expressed, they are likely to be of little value. The idea that some opinions are well informed and some poorly informed is an important one for citizens in democratic societies because they must form their own opinions based on those expressed by others in the public arena. Distinguishing between legitimate, substantive argument as opposed to, say, passionate rhetoric or media-savvy linguistic legerdemain is an important, indeed an essential, skill that does not come naturally but must be learned. It is but one of many stepping stones on the pathway to becoming wise.

Wisdom, too, is something that we acquire, not something we are born with. Citizens cannot vote wisely if they are not wise. Schools cannot in and of themselves make anyone wise, but they can provide a foundation and some basic building blocks that will help people become wise. Schools can help equip us with the skills to search out answers to questions we may have concerning, for example, matters of public policy. Schools can teach us to distinguish between what is and what is not validated, useful information. The difference is important.

It is a responsibility of all citizens in a democracy to protect their individual and collective rights and freedoms. People cannot do this if they do not know what those rights and freedoms are, if they do not understand how those rights and freedoms play out in reality, if they do not recognize the forces that threaten those rights and freedoms. For classroom teachers alone, the implications of these few words, if fully understood and taken seriously, are far-reaching. For all of us, as a nation, they help to proscribe a clear mission for our schools, colleges, and universities.

But our educational institutions also have contributions to make at a more personal level. Julie Underwood has stated that when our democracy was forged, "Strong character and moral virtue were considered an essential part of good citizenship." But what does this mean for a society as diverse as ours? In his discussion of the necessary characteristics of a democratic people, Roger Soder begins by suggesting trust, exchange, and social capital. "These three conditions are closely related," Soder explains, "as are the dispositions necessary to secure them." When he speaks of trust, Soder means that democratic societies need to "encourage as a disposition a general willingness to trust" and that this willingness needs also to be "tempered by a prudent skepticism." With respect to exchange, Soder suggests, "We must encourage people to engage in exchange, honor the obligations exchange implies, and be mindful of the dangers of unbalanced exchange." Recognizing the need for the kinds of social and political skills—collectively referred to as *social capital*—that make it possible for people to work together to understand problems and develop solutions, Soder states that social capital needs to be understood "as a tool, skill, and process" available to everyone.[7]

Additional characteristics of a democratic people include a respect for equal justice under the law. "We must encourage respect for the law," Soder writes, "even when decisions go against perceived self-interest." Respect for civil discourse is another important characteristic. People need "to be willing to entertain propositions, consider evidence, and accept ambiguity as inevitable." There needs to be a willingness to recognize the inherent tension between our own self-interests and those of society at large "as a positive good rather than a problem to be solved." In other words, Soder explains, "People need to reject the tendency to resolve the tension by trying to choose either one or the other."[8] (This is an important and difficult topic that we shall return to shortly.)

Free and open inquiry is another characteristic important for democracy's citizens. "We must encourage critical inquiry as a personal and civic virtue," Soder writes. "We must therefore encourage a willingness to be a minority of one and acceptance of democracy as a manifestation, in the words of [John] Dewey, of the 'capacity of the intelligence of the common man to respond with commonsense to the free play of facts and ideas which are secured by effective guarantees of free inquiry, free assembly, and free communication.'"[9]

There is a difference between a persuaded audience and a thoughtful public. Democracies "must encourage a willingness to select and support leaders and representatives who will not pander to ephemeral public tastes or the immediately gratifying," Soder explains, adding that "if we have venal, calculating, servile, or otherwise unprincipled leaders, we must look to our own character and not transfer the blame to those who take advantage of our ignorance and lack of virtue." This means, among other things, that "given the threats to a democracy posed by at least some of the highly ambitious, we must be able to distinguish between those who value their reputations for probity and ability to benefit the community—for such valuation will temper their ambitions—and those who want only to benefit themselves."[10]

As suggested earlier, a knowledge of rights is also essential to a democratic citizenry, as is an understanding of the concept of freedom that does not and cannot exist without some kind of order, without rules, without there being limits to curtail certain kinds of behavior, and without some form of authority to assist in maintaining a balance between the two.[11]

It is not our intent to suggest that the characteristics Soder discusses are the *only* characteristics necessary to a democratic citizenry, nor is it to be assumed that Soder's list is definitive. But Soder does provide a useful summation of what we mean when we speak of *democratic character*.

Historical Roots of Schooling and Democracy

These ideas were not taken lightly by the framers of the Constitution, who recognized them as integral to a democratic system of governance. The strength of Jefferson's conviction in this regard surfaced when he was asked what he would like to have inscribed on his tombstone. Making no mention of "his two-term presidency, his acquisition of the Louisiana Territory, his founding of the Democratic Party," or other major achievements, Jefferson instead asked to be remembered for "his authorship of the Declaration of Independence, his writing of the Virginia Statute of Religious Freedom, and his founding of the University of Virginia." His reasoning was simple, as Benjamin Barber explains: "Without public education for all citizens, Jefferson did not see how there could be a democratic politics at all.

Without citizens there could be no republic, and without education there could be no citizens."[12]

Jefferson was not alone in harboring such beliefs. In fact, many of Jefferson's ideas have roots dating back to America's colonial days "when John Adams of Massachusetts boasted that the Commonwealth's schools tutored every young man in citizenship with a ubiquity that put 'literate' England to shame."[13] Political scientist Nathan Tarcov notes that Adams saw republican government itself as being "a form of education that introduces knowledge among the people, inspires them with a conscious dignity befitting freemen, encourages a general emulation and elevation of sentiment that make the people brave and enterprising as well as sober, industrious, and frugal."[14] Adams believed that "[l]aws for the liberal education of youth, especially of the lower class of people, are so extremely wise and useful, that to a humane and generous mind, no expense for this purpose would be thought extravagant."[15]

Earlier we noted that other voices expressed similar sentiments. Alexis de Tocqueville wrote of an "apprenticeship of liberty."[16] The Common School Movement saw in public education a civic purpose that guided the educational practices of schools and colleges throughout the nineteenth century. "Not just the land-grant colleges," Barber explains,

> but nearly every higher educational institution founded in the eighteenth and nineteenth centuries—religious as well as secular, private no less than public—counted among its leading founding principles a dedication to training competent and responsible citizens. Rights were understood to be tied to responsibilities, the freedom to live well and prosper was seen as a product of civic obligations discharged with vigor, and the security of the private sector was thought to depend on the robustness of the public sector.[17]

In a country that was sparsely populated and rather homogenous, the mission of schooling was more straightforward than it is today. "The Christian faith and the laws of community living were seen virtually as one," John Goodlad reminds us. Parallel curricula were followed at home, at church, and in the schools. "But the siren call of freedom was to attract to this land those of other faiths, no faith, other beliefs and even other gods," Goodlad writes. "The mix was, in time, to sorely test and strain the great democratic experiment."[18]

These early schools worked fairly well when most who attended (virtually all of whom were of European ancestry) had much in common and everyone shared much the same values. But an increasingly diversified public soon rendered the concept of the common school obsolete. "Common schools were conceived as places where civic virtue was passed on to the next generation," Julie Underwood explains. "Public schools were created as places where a diverse nation of immigrants could come together to learn how to be a democracy."[19] Although there have been a few notable exceptions, by and large our nation has never come close to perfecting public schooling. Our early schools were a far cry from being places that nurtured children and ensured equity and access to all. And despite our high ideals and good intentions, current practices also leave much to be desired.

This shift from the common school to the public school reflected not so much a shift in purpose but rather a shift in how we went about achieving that purpose. Schools still had to do most of the same things they had done before, but they had to do some things differently because the public they were now serving was changing. If, at the time, the Agenda for Education in a Democracy had existed and the idea of simultaneous renewal had been available, both would have been as useful then as they are today. Change has always been a part of schools and schooling. This is why effective methods of bringing about change need to be incorporated within the school system itself, thus making change part of the process instead of a series of disruptions that must be hurdled.

The increasing diversity of America's citizenry would present not only problems but opportunities as well. Because ideally "public schools must educate all comers, they offer all young people the opportunity to build their citizenship skills, thereby helping to ensure that future voters and leaders will come from all walks of life," Julie Underwood writes. "In public schools with diverse student populations, students have the opportunity to hear different points of view, to disagree amicably, and to reach livable compromises. In other words, public schools are the places where we learn to get along with one another."[20]

As American society grew increasingly complex, as more and more people left rural areas and migrated into urban centers, as industrialization and mechanization gained a greater foothold, and as our population increased and diversified, schools were asked time and again to shoulder responsibilities that were far beyond those they had traditionally assumed. The attention spans of students did not correspondingly increase during this period, nor did the number of hours in a day, nor the energy level of their teachers. So something else had to "give" to accommodate these new demands. Unfortunately, civics courses were often among the first to be sacrificed.

They were not, for the most part, missed. In fact, such changes in curriculum went largely unnoticed and gradually became institutionalized. As far as most people were concerned, schools were schools were schools, and they never appeared to change much one way or the other.

But in society at large, significant changes did take place. "Most adult Americans no longer live to any significant degree as citizens," Westbrook points out, "and hence it is not surprising that few feel a compelling need to educate American children for public life."[21] In other words, while our schools have not entirely lived up to their civic responsibilities, it is also the case that we, the public, have failed to adequately support the schools in this crucial mission.

"A political democracy requires for its sustenance the reiteration of truths and widespread allegiance to them. The more comprehensive these truths and the more commonly shared, the more sustaining the democracy subscribing to them will be."[22] In light of these statements, it would seem that in recent times there has been an increase in the weight of our moral responsibilities with respect to education for democracy.

The Moral Responsibility for Democracy Education

Some have argued that schooling should be a minor priority given the many other matters we deal with as a society. What about child care? What about health care? What about domestic security? What about our economic infrastructure? Some have argued that there is little to be gained by investing valuable time, energy, and resources on schooling for democracy—a nice idea, but not an essential one—when so much of our political and social infrastructure is in flux. But this is criticism based on an incomplete understanding of the circumstances, and perhaps societal disarray is a consequence of our inattention to education for democracy and the role of schooling in it.

This kind of criticism is directed primarily at the disarray itself. It fails to consider adequately the many difficult steps that must be taken to ensure a reasonably safe, healthy, and productive life for everyone. We use the word *reasonably* because, given the discouraging realities that will inevitably be confronted, higher expectations are less likely to inspire than they are to produce greater disillusionment. Therefore, the prospect of a good and meaningful life for each and every one of us must for now remain a goal for the long term.[23]

This is not to say that by accomplishing one thing we accomplish the other. Democratic schooling does not guarantee a democratic society. But a nation cannot have or sustain for long a democratic society without some form of democratic schooling.

The idea of a good and meaningful life for all has been around, it seems, in various guises since time immemorial. Yet it remains in many respects a radical idea. The U.S. Constitution speaks specifically of "life, liberty and the pursuit of happiness." These are the ideals at the heart of American democracy, itself so radical an idea that Tocqueville termed it "an experiment." Democracy exists in large part because of a persistent and widespread belief that everyone should be given access to the good life regardless of individual circumstances of birth, religion, race, or socioeconomic class. But simply "having democracy" does not necessarily provide everyone with access to the "good life," however we choose to define it. This is where education comes into play. For those who are not, by virtue of wealth and status, born into the good life, education is our best hope for providing opportunities to them that otherwise might not exist.

But education plays another role in our pursuit of the good life. As an "icon of equality, mobility, and hope in our society," educators Linda Darling-Hammond and Jacqueline Ancess state, "public education has become the passport to the American dream." They remind us that the purposes of public education in a democratic society were, according to Thomas Jefferson, twofold: first, "to prepare all individuals for citizenship by developing within them the capacity for full and intelligent participation in the processes of deliberation necessary for self-rule," and second, "to identify and develop responsible leadership from the talents and abilities of individuals rather than from family or group privilege, economic wealth, religion, or race."[24] Clearly, given this very public role of education in a democracy, "the state would have to provide all individuals with access to educational opportunities sufficient to prepare them for full and intelligent citizenship."[25] This assertion places a tremendous moral responsibility on America's schools and educators. It states that as a nation we have a moral obligation to prepare our young for participation in the complex system of social and political organization that we call democracy. To deny this, or to fail to do all that is within our power to achieve this, would not only be a gross injustice to future generations, but also a denial of our own national heritage.

From the outset, our nation's educators have employed a language of schooling that emphasizes educating for responsibility, whether as a parent, worker, or citizen. While the idea of educating for self-realization has been around for quite some time, it did not gain real prominence until well into the twentieth century. Today these competing strains of thought represent quite different attitudes concerning how our schools ought to operate and what they ought to try to accomplish. As educational philosopher Barry L. Bull explains,

> [Americans] often evince what appears to be a self-contradictory attitude toward public schools. On the one hand, we expect schools to discipline the nation's children vigorously—to constrain their thoughts and especially their behavior for the present and to produce loyal citizens and willing workers for the future. On the other hand, we want children (especially our own) to have the chance to express and develop their individual potential in school and to emerge with a personal strength of character and a freedom of intelligence that will enable them to lead rich and independent adult lives.[26]

Bull notes that our ideas about the moral purposes of government strongly shape our ideas about the public mission of schooling. Such a dichotomy can be overly simplified to suggest that it reflects two competing views of governance: laissez-faire versus authoritarianism. In this conceptualization, proponents of a laissez-faire ideology would argue that schools must protect the young from a process of collective enculturation, while those who lean toward a more authoritarian ideology would tend to see education as a necessary process of systematic enculturation. Such oversimplified definitions would lead us to conclude that Americans can share no coherent view concerning the moral responsibilities of schooling.

But this notion that there exists a dual attitude toward schools resulting from competing ideological ideas about government and governance is inadequate. It assumes a historically nonexistent polarity that, regardless of which side of the equation one finds oneself on, implies commonly shared ideas about both constraint and independence with regard to the public purposes of schooling. Bull summarizes the matter this way: "A liberal society's educational goals, in the broadest terms, are simultaneously to promote each person's independence in the formation of his or her vision of the good and to promote a common recognition of one's obligation to respect and secure a similar independence for others."[27]

The dichotomy addressed in the preceding paragraph reflects an often-misunderstood tension that is at the heart of human existence. World historian Alan Wood has written extensively on this topic. Wood concludes "that freedom and authority are potentially lethal by themselves but an elixir of long life when complemented by each other. Freedom and authority are related to each other not as enemies but as allies, not as antagonists but as partners. They fulfill their purpose only when they are in balance with each other, not when they are in opposition to each other. Each derives its essential meaning, moreover, from its relation to the other."[28]

Freedom can be viewed in two ways: as negative freedom and as positive freedom. Negative freedom reflects an absence of constraint. It is the kind of freedom that supports ideas of autonomy and rugged individualism. Its counterpart, positive freedom, is rooted in our social and cultural bonds and concerns itself not with eliminating constraints but with fulfilling potential. "The educational process," Wood explains,

> insofar as it is carried out in the context of schools, expresses this formative, informative, and transformative purpose. One starts with what is and moves toward what might be, keeping in mind that the ultimate aim is to liberate students from ignorance and prepare them for life in a community. Education in a democracy is the carrier of freedom, but freedom of a particular kind. To be fully human means to accept limitations on one's negative freedoms in order to realize more fully one's positive freedoms.[29]

It is difficult to step back from the realm of ideas and ideals and think seriously about the "real world" implications of educating for a democratic citizenry, but to appreciate fully the complex dimensions of the challenges such an undertaking entails, we need to try to do so. Attempting to teach well a diverse third-grade class of children—with all their varied life experiences; cultural, religious, and social backgrounds; differing belief systems; learning abilities; skill levels; and dreams, fears, hopes, and ambitions—how to read, write, and do arithmetic is, in and of itself, a formidable and daunting challenge, one that not many adults in our population would willingly take on. But imagine the difficulties of also attempting to cultivate each student's independent formation of her or his own notion of the good life while simultaneously working to develop a shared recognition of each student's obligation to make it possible for others to do the same. As Barry L. Bull explains,

> Liberalism's central commitment to facilitating the realization of each person's vision of the good life, whatever that vision turns out to be, has traditionally been taken to require a liberal society to guarantee each citizen's freedom to act as his or her view of the good dictates. However, because individuals' views of the good may differ, one person's acting freely in pursuit of her good may impede another's freedom to pursue his good. Since liberalism is committed to all people's pursuit of their goods, any liberal theory must specify the morally legitimate limits of each person's freedom.[30]

In an authoritarian society, one is simply provided with a set of rules and expected to conform to them. Schooling here could clearly be limited to a set of basic skills. Democracy is a far more complex proposition that requires all citizens to share in the moral responsibilities of governance, both with respect to their own individual behaviors and to the extent necessary to ensure the well-being of others and the common good. While the responsibility of preparing youngsters to participate effectively in such a system of governance can seem daunting, getting "back to the basics" is not an acceptable alternative. Unfortunately, that's the direction in which most schools are now headed.

Getting back to the basics (that is, teaching basic scholastic skills and standardized subject matter) may make youngsters better classroom students and perhaps, in some cases, better workers. Such an approach, however, is insufficient to create and sustain a healthy democracy. As history has taught us time and again, even under the most ideal conditions, democracies are fragile, and they will surely perish if a deliberate and concerted effort is not made to sustain them.

In a quite fundamental way, that burden falls most heavily on the shoulders of teachers. Public schooling is the only educative experience shared by almost every single person in a free society. No institution exists in the modern world other than our schools that can begin to fulfill this most essential and fundamental responsibility. Democracy's tomorrow depends very much on what goes on in classrooms today.

Rethinking Our Priorities

The preceding discussion raises the question, Why should schools be asked to assume the responsibility for democracy education? For example, why shouldn't all adults share in the task of educating the young for democratic citizenship? To an extent, adults often do precisely this, usually unwittingly, and this very lack of intent can present serious problems. The way adults conduct themselves, the values they espouse (actions being louder than words), the rules they make and how they make them, and many other behaviors present the young with a particular (and not always ethical) view of the world, including certain ideas about how society works and the ends it serves.

As often as not, such an informal education is largely as unintended as its consequences. There is no organizing process involved; no lesson plans are prepared. Processes of engagement and thoughtful reflection have little, if any, role to play. There is no formal evaluative process by which successes and failures can be gauged (until long after the real world consequences have made themselves known). It amounts to something on the order of giving a group of stockbrokers a failed aircraft engine to tinker with. They might, if only inadvertently, actually make the thing run. But who wants to take the test flight? More to the point, do we really want these folks in charge of engine maintenance for the whole airline industry? Wouldn't we do better to hire trained, competent airline mechanics to do the job? In reality, this is of course precisely what we do, begging this question: Are airplanes any more important than democracy? Wouldn't it make sense to try to achieve a corresponding degree of competence in our collective decision-making processes? In other words, simply leaving education for democracy in the hands of anyone who cares to take a stab at it or, possibly worse, leaving youngsters to try to ferret out what lessons they can from the tumult of the world around them is so unpredictable and so haphazard an approach as to be more threatening than beneficial.

The problems of educating for democratic citizenry are especially acute when it comes to the very young. These youngsters lack not only "a vision of the good," Bull observes,

> but even the general capacity to choose and hold such a vision. . . . These children need to establish in some systematic way a coherent cultural foundation that will enable them eventually to develop a genuinely self-chosen vision of the good. If taught indiscriminately by any and all adults, however, children may fail to develop any systematic foundation for becoming their own persons. Unrestricted freedoms to teach and learn from others, which are important for adults' being and becoming their own persons, can actually impede children's development toward that very goal.[31]

The liberal function of teachers in a democratic society is to develop the abilities of their students to choose and cultivate visions of the good life while simultaneously preparing them for full participation in adult society. Central to such preparation is the ability to exercise one's basic freedoms responsibly and without unjustly preventing others from doing the same. This requires that individual students develop a degree of healthy autonomy, independence of judgment, strength of character, and a measure of self-understanding. It is from such a foundation that individuals can begin to acquire purpose by choosing among the various visions of good available within the constructs of one's society. To be legitimately free, such choosing must be done intelligently and with a reasonably good understanding of the full range of possible alternatives. There must also be present within the individual a fairly well-developed sense of justice. That sense of justice must be in keeping with the fundamental belief systems and commitments of a liberal society. Such a sense of justice will not only allow one to pursue appropriately one's own vision of the good, but will also enable one to do so within the greater scheme of cooperation that is necessary to ensure that others may do likewise.

There is a lack of precision in the descriptions of the qualities discussed in the preceding paragraph: a "healthy autonomy," "a measure of self-understanding," "a fairly well-developed sense of justice," and so on. This imprecision is both intentional and unavoidable. These are at best extremely difficult qualities to try to define and measure. They are also qualities that vary significantly from one individual to another. As individuals, we cannot all share the same sense of justice or be equal in our autonomy or have the same sense of self-understanding. Moreover, how these qualities can be developed most effectively will differ greatly from one person to another. Once we realize this, it becomes evident that any standardized, prepackaged, across-the-board curricular or pedagogical approach is bound to be inadequate. Such an approach cannot begin to adapt adequately to the infinite idiosyncrasies of a diverse student population. It also dramatically underscores the need for competent, well-trained teachers who must be trusted with a considerable degree of autonomy and provided with the conditions, tools, and materials they need to do this difficult and essential work. Benjamin Barber nicely illustrates the importance, complexity, and challenges of such an undertaking. Drawing on the teachings of ancient Athens, Barber writes that the

> lesson for modern societies like America that affect to be free is that to teach liberty is, first of all, to teach time: both past and future. To teach time is not simply to teach conventional history or some high school version of pop futurology. It is to transmit a sense of our story as a people—the narrative of our struggle to become a people. It is to investigate the course of liberty as aspiration and the course of liberty as a historically realized (or historically unrealized) actuality. To teach liberty is thus to teach imagination. It is to teach creativity, to teach responsibility, to teach autonomy, and to teach embeddedness. Its vessel is not so much curriculum as an approach to curriculum: one that is interdisciplinary, civic-minded, and critical; one never too far removed from the story . . . of what it means to be an American.[32]

Barber's words resonate with those of Barry Bull when Bull argues that as a liberal society our educational goals ought to be to "promote each person's independence in the formation of his or her vision of the good and to promote a common recognition of one's obligation to respect and secure a similar independence for others." Both of these writers view our nation's schools with a level of sophistication and reverence often lacking in what passes for contemporary discussion of the subject. Rather than viewing our schools as blunt instruments to be used to instill some crude Pavlovian patriotism in the hearts and minds of our youth, Barber, Bull, and others from whose works we have drawn place our schools at the very center of American democracy and assign to them the most crucial of responsibilities.

The importance of the role that schooling must play in a democratic society cannot be overemphasized. Without a solid educational foundation, the democratic state becomes as aimless and vulnerable as a rudderless ship in a storm-tossed sea. Yes, child care is an important concern; so is health care, so is domestic security, so is the stability of our economic infrastructure, and so are a good many other problems we must face. But this does not mean that we can allow schooling to become a lesser priority. Not only do schools have an essential role to play in the development, health, and well-being of our nation's young, but they are also the only institutions we have for rigorously promoting and sustaining our social and political democracy, which in turn is responsible for improving child care, health care, domestic security, and so on. As important as these other problems are, none is so important that we can justify sacrificing our democracy in order to try to address it.

To really understand the weight of this argument, we might do well simply to look at things from an opposing perspective. Such a perspective would argue that as a society we should not try to ensure a reasonably safe, healthy, and productive life for one another. It would argue that those who are not born to the good life by virtue of wealth and status should be denied potentially crucial opportunities to try to improve their lot. It would argue that Thomas Jefferson was wrong, that we share no collective responsibility for preparing our young for citizenship by developing within them the ability to participate intelligently in the processes of deliberation essential to self-rule; that we share no responsibility to try to identify and develop competent leadership from the talents and abilities of individuals, but rather should look to family or group privilege, wealth, religion, race, or some similar criteria for such leadership. Such a perspective would argue that promoting each individual's independence in the formation of his or her vision of the good as well as developing a shared recognition of our obligations to respect and secure a similar independence for others ought not be foremost among our educational priorities.

This opposing perspective would suggest that schools need not trouble themselves with promoting and sustaining our democracy, that somehow someone else or some other institution will miraculously take care of that. It would argue that it is unnecessary or inappropriate for schools to work to develop in their students independence of judgment, strength of character, and self-understanding. Learning what one's basic freedoms are and how to exercise those freedoms responsibly without unjustly preventing others from doing the same would be assumed to be inappropriate subject matter for our nation's young. Finally, this alternative view would argue that our schools should not try to examine the course of liberty as both aspiration and actuality, or try to provide the young with a sense of our historic struggle to become a people, or teach creativity, or responsibility, or autonomy, or what Benjamin Barber terms "embeddedness." It is difficult to imagine that many of us would embrace such a bleak and uninspiring role for our schools.

Such an approach would not be without its advocates. It would, for instance, greatly simplify the work of schooling: reading, writing, and a little arithmetic and science would constitute pretty much the entire scope of the curriculum. It would have universal appeal: the same model would serve a democracy or a dictatorship equally well. It would also remove most of the moral burden of schooling as we have articulated it. In fact, the need for skilled, caring, competent teachers would be dramatically reduced (if not eliminated altogether). The bulk of the curriculum could be turned over to computer programs that would drill students in the basics of spelling, punctuation, addition, subtraction, and general reading comprehension. We might not develop much in the way of a democratic citizenry, but we'd have a nation of well-prepared takers of standardized tests.

Clearly the moral aspects of schooling are not confined solely to our nation's classrooms, nor are they to be borne solely on the shoulders of our nation's teachers, though to be sure teachers do and must bear a special moral burden in this regard. America's public schools are the moral responsibility of the public at large. If—in our roles as parents, voters, taxpayers, teachers, administrators, politicians, or other—we fail to live up to our moral responsibilities with respect to public schooling, we not only fail ourselves, but we also fail our young, future generations of Americans, and ultimately we fail our country, our democracy, and our way of life. If this is not a moral issue, it is hard to imagine what else could be.

Good schools will not and cannot guarantee a good and healthy democracy. There are simply too many other forces at play, and democracy is far too fragile and has far too many enemies. But a democracy is much less likely to exist in the absence of a good, effective, and widely supported system of public education. That education must cultivate in its students the skills and wisdom to deal peacefully and justly with the often unforeseen problems that our future will most assuredly hold. Kenneth Sirotnik nicely summarizes our situation when he writes:

> America is a collection of multiple communities defined by different interests, races, ethnicities, regions, economic stratifications, religions, and so forth. Celebrating these differences is part of what makes this nation great. But there is a community—a moral community—that transcends the special interests of individuals, families, groups, that stands for what this nation is all about: liberty *and justice* for all. This "community," of course, is an abstraction. It is a "moral ecology" held together by a political democracy and the fundamental values embedded in the system.[33]

No political and social system as ambitious, complex, and idealistic as a democracy can ever hope to survive—let alone thrive—without citizens equipped with the knowledge, skills, and dispositions necessary to sustain it. Schools play an essential role in creating and sustaining such citizens. If, as Julie Underwood described them earlier in this chapter, schools are "the places where we learn to get along with one another," they also form the bedrock of the moral community on which our liberties, security, and even our lives depend.

Chapter Four

An Essential Narrative for Schooling

Reform, reform, don't speak to me of reform.
We have enough problems already.
—*Lord Thomas Macaulay, Nineteenth-Century*
British Politician

In 1961, democracy advocate Robert Alan Haber wrote of what he described as a "qualitative problem." Students on college campuses across the nation were only then in their lives beginning to grapple with the idea that "democracy is based on the idea of a 'political' public—a body that shares a range of common values and commitments, an institutional pattern of interaction and an image of themselves as a functioning community. *We do not now have such a public in America.*"[1] Haber's statement raises a number of important questions. Where do these "common values and commitments" come from? How do they come to be? How does a next generation learn what they are and what they mean? How do people create and sustain "an institutional pattern of interaction and an image of themselves as a functioning community"? In short, how does a society create the "'political' public" that democracy requires?

Preceding chapters have noted that schools are commonly called on to perform a variety of functions, among them to develop personal, social, vocational, and academic competencies. But to what larger end? Is it essential that children go to school in order to learn how to get along with one another? Are we, as a species, not capable of developing social competencies without formalized schooling? Do we really have to go to school to learn to become competent workers? And of what use are academic competencies once we leave the sanctified world of academe? Why do we feel we have to have a formalized system of public schools? Toward what end should they exist if we are to have them?

Without a broadly and overtly recognized and agreed upon mission, schooling becomes an empty vessel. It exists, but without real meaning or purpose. It exists simply *because* it exists, not because society recognizes that it *needs* to exist. Most people, when asked why we have a system of public education, would likely answer that we have schools so young people can learn reading, writing, and the fundamentals of such subjects as science and mathematics. Some may even mention history, art, and literature. When asked what end this learning serves, most people would answer that it is "so graduates can get a good job." If one doubts the accuracy of this assessment, one need only review the rhetoric of schooling in recent decades. While every president in the past fifty years has talked about the importance of education, how many have suggested that schools might do more than prepare students for more schooling and produce competent workers?

There is nothing wrong with having a competent workforce or with students getting higher scores on standardized tests, even though the latter accomplishment correlates with little other than further test performance. But do we really need an elaborate system of taxpayer-supported public education in order to do these things?

Getting higher test scores is virtually an end in and of itself. Such scores do not predict or correspond to success in such things as personal relationships, good work, play, or sound mental and physical health. For the most part, they become meaningless as soon as a student leaves the classroom. Can we really justify investing enormous amounts of time, energy, money, and resources just to produce a nation of top-notch test takers?

To have a competent workforce is a reasonable goal for any society, democratic or otherwise. But is it suitable as a comprehensive mission for public education? Should our highest hopes and aspirations for our sons and daughters be merely that they grow up to become competent workers? Neil Postman shares our view that something is lacking in so limited and unimaginative a vision. Postman writes that this "narrative consists of such an uninspiring set of assumptions that it is hardly noticed as a narrative at all. But we may count it as one, largely because so many people believe it to be the preeminent reason for schooling. It may properly go by the name of the god of Economic Utility."[2]

If we are to understand the recent history of schooling in the United States as well as the reality of much of what schooling consists of today, we must become familiar with this "god of Economic Utility." "As its name suggests," Postman continues,

> it is a passionless god, cold and severe. But it makes a promise, and not a trivial one. Addressing the young, it offers a covenant of sorts with them: If you will pay attention in school, and do your homework, and score well on tests, and behave yourself, you will be rewarded with a well-paying job when you are done. Its driving idea is that the purpose of schooling is to prepare children for competent entry into the economic life of a community. It follows from this that any school activity not designed to further this end is seen as a frill or an ornament—which is to say, a waste of valuable time.[3]

This narrative of Economic Utility arises from a particular worldview that can be said to date back to humankind's earliest times. Like any creature, humans are strongly motivated to provide themselves with material sustenance. We need to eat. We need shelter. We seek warmth, comfort, and security. That we ought to share with one another the knowledge and skills to sustain our existence seems a reasonable proposition.

Moreover, this economic narrative has a somewhat spiritual aspect to it as well. It is cobbled together from a variety of sources, such as the tale of the Protestant ethic and the writings of Karl

Marx and Adam Smith. "The story tells us that we are first and foremost economic creatures," Postman explains,

> and that our sense of worth and purpose is to be found in our capac-
> ity to secure material benefits. This is one reason why the schooling
> of women, until recently, was not considered of high value. Accord-
> ing to this god, you *are* what you do for a living—a rather problem-
> atic conception of human nature even if one could be assured of a
> stimulating and bountiful job. Nevertheless, that assurance is given
> through a clear delineation of good and evil. Goodness inheres in
> productivity, efficiency, and organization; evil in inefficiency and
> sloth. Like any self-respecting god, this one withholds its favor from
> those who are evil and bestows it abundantly on those who are good.
>
> The story goes on to preach that America is not so much a
> culture as it is an economy, and that the vitality of any nation's econ-
> omy rests on high standards of achievement and rigorous discipline in
> schools. There is little evidence (that is to say, none) that the produc-
> tivity of a nation's economy is related to the quality of its schooling.[4]

Naturally, those few who reap the vast majority of the benefits (largely political and economic) to be gained by promoting this narrative will do their utmost to see to it that the god of Economic Utility continues to reign supreme. It is, after all, in *their* best inter-ests to do so. But for the rest of us, and not least of all for our children, who surely see themselves as more than mere cogs in a vast industrial machine, it is a narrative that leaves a great deal to be desired. If, for example, there were much truth to it, the major-ity of our nation's graduates would be sitting behind desks in posh corporate offices while raking in millions of dollars in salaries, stock options, and bonuses, instead of working behind the counter at McDonald's or the local department store for the minimum wage. The god of Economic Utility is not simply uninspiring, but decep-tive and, for the most part, fraudulent as well.

It is troubling—or at least it should be to most people—that political speeches, television commercials, and vast segments of the mass media work relentlessly to advocate this bleak narrative. It is perhaps even more troubling that many of our most prominent leaders—people who really should know better—are no less culpable. We have to wonder why this is the case, "why this god has so much strength, why the preparation for making a living, *which is well served by any decent education*, should be assigned a metaphysical position of such high station," Postman writes. He then proposes that "the reason is that the god of Economic Utility is coupled with another god, one with a smiling face and one that provides an answer to the question, If I get a good job, then what?" This, Postman tells us, is "the god of Consumership, whose basic moral axiom is expressed in the slogan 'Whoever dies with the most toys wins'—that is to say, goodness inheres in those who buy things; evil in those who do not. The similarity between this god and the god of Economic Utility is obvious, but with this difference: The latter postulates that you *are* what you do for a living; the former that you *are* what you accumulate."[5] This is, of course, also the predominant message of all popular American media. It is a message created and perpetuated largely by corporations and their financial beneficiaries (which usually include politicians) for obvious and already-stated reasons.

If the mission of schooling is simply to perpetuate the narrative of Economic Utility, feeding of course the god of Consumership, then schooling has little of real substance to offer the very people it purports to serve. Not only is the god of Economic Utility a false god whose promises are largely misleading and empty, it is a superficial and uninspiring one as well. And given the unwavering support and commitment this god receives from both the mainstream media and our nation's political leaders, it need not rely on our schools in order to thrive. If vocational preparation and economic indoctrination are to be the driving forces behind public education, then we hardly need such an expensive and elaborate system. A loose arrangement of corporation-sponsored boot camps would suffice.

Once again we must ask of education: Toward what end?

The Failings of Reform

As successful as the narrative of Economic Utility has been in achieving a seemingly ubiquitous and unassailable foothold in the American psyche, the recent history of schooling nevertheless suggests widespread dissatisfaction with the status quo and an inexorable determination to put things right. There is a popular saying that goes, "Don't mess with success," yet it would seem to even the most casual observer, when confronted with the recurrent school reform movements of recent decades, that this is precisely what our leaders would have us do. Somehow, for these folks, success just hasn't been good enough.

It would not be inaccurate to describe the recent history of American education as one of one reform movement after another. And each of these movements is in turn followed by declarations of failure. These declarations then provoke yet another round of reforms, which result in more failures and calls for more reforms. To try to understand this repetition, let us briefly consider the meaning and implications of the word *reform*.

Whether we speak of reforming schools, reforming the economy, reforming the political system, or even reforming the world, we are suggesting—among other things—that the object of attention has gone wrong, gone bad, gone astray. To state that reform is in order is, in effect, to condemn that which is to be reformed. It suggests that intervention from outside forces is *the* necessary and desirable approach to solving problems, real or imagined.

Reform asserts that solutions will not and cannot arise from within (in the case of schooling) the system and that regulatory mechanisms do not exist to enable educators to find solutions to their own problems within what ought to be their sphere of influence. In other words, to call for reform is to tar with the brush of failure that which is to be reformed, whatever it may be. Reform is a last-resort action prompted by crisis. It is an intervention that automatically places the reformers, whoever they may be, in a relationship of authority over those targeted for reform.

In the case of public education in the United States, calls for reform have been invoked by one generation of leaders after another for the better part of a century. We could try to trace this history of reform movements back to its origins (however *origins* might be defined), but such a lengthy and involved digression would serve little purpose here. What is important to note is that these reform movements generated from afar have been radically different from the kinds of local dialogue and debate aimed at improving public education that once were the norm. Such dialogues and debates were, in effect, ongoing conversations that involved, almost exclusively, parents and teachers within the same local community. This kind of ongoing discussion is healthy and to be encouraged. It is part of what should be a conscious and sustained effort to provide the best education possible. The world is not static; nor should education be. An educational system that does not have ongoing means and methods for critical self-examination and transformation is hardly worthy of the name.

The more recent movements we are talking about here have been major (usually national) efforts that, in the name of reform, have promised to radically remake public education to serve particular ends or address perceived failings (which invariably turn out to be political, economic, or both). Such reform movements are not confined to a bygone era. They are as prevalent and persistent today as they were fifty years ago—and show no signs of abating. In fact, much of the history that follows may strike the reader as eerily familiar.

It is particularly discouraging to note that no magnitude of failure seems able to persuade us to get off the treadmill of reform and seek more promising alternatives. This situation is all the more irksome given that the leaders of these reform efforts would have us believe that public education in this country has been in a state of crisis, requiring measures of immediate and draconian intervention, for something on the order of a hundred years, despite our nation's many social, economic, and political achievements during that time.

For students, teachers, parents, and schools, not only have the reform movements of recent decades done more damage than good, but their proponents have completely ignored the fact that public expectations for what schooling ought to try to accomplish has itself changed little. As we have pointed out elsewhere, "The dozen or so goals [deemed appropriate to American education] that surface again and again in commissioned reports and district guidelines for schools have consistently embraced personal, social, vocational, and academic attributes."[6] In other words, in terms of a generalized mandate, the mission of schooling is quite clear—and has been for a long time. The mission of schooling is not that of a machine that advances the nation's role in the global economy.

Reform Part One: New Priorities

In the 1950s, American schools (and for that matter, much of American society) enjoyed a period of postwar growth, prosperity, and optimism that was the envy of many nations around the world. In many ways, the United States seemed to be *the* model of educational success. Visitors came from afar to observe and study innovative educational practices.

Despite this success, however, our nation faced enormous problems. Racism, sexism, and homophobia, for example, continued to plague both our schools and our society. We were involved in a war in Korea and were soon to become involved in one in Vietnam. McCarthyism was taking its poisonous toll. On a global scale, the Cold War pitted the United States and its allies against the former Union of Soviet Socialist Republics (USSR) and its allies.

Nevertheless, for many people, the general outlook was a positive one. There was a sense of forward movement, the air was charged with possibility, change was in the wind, and movements were under way to address a myriad of ills. In the wake of two world wars, real and dramatic social, economic, and political progress seemed at hand. Our experiment in universal schooling appeared to be working.

For America's schools, change arrived abruptly on November 3, 1957, when the Soviets launched a satellite named *Sputnik* that carried a small dog named Laika. This flight was felt, at the time, to represent an enormous scientific and technological advance on the part of the Soviets. As David Halberstam has written,

> The success of *Sputnik* seemed to herald a kind of technological Pearl Harbor, which in fact was exactly what physicist Edward Teller called it. A Democratic legislative aid wrote a paper for Lyndon Johnson showing him that this issue could take him to the White House. (He was wrong.) Some saw it as a rebuke to America's material self-indulgence. . . . Suddenly, it seemed as if America were undergoing a national crisis of confidence. Admiral Hyman Rickover criticized the American school system. A book called *Why Johnny Can't Read—and What You Can Do About It*, which had appeared two years earlier to little attention, suddenly became a smash best-seller. The president of Harvard, Nathan Pusey, was moved to declare that a greater percentage of the GNP should go to education.[7]

As a result of the Soviet launch of *Sputnik*, many political and educational leaders felt that, as a nation, the United States was technologically falling behind the USSR—and thus losing the arms race and quite possibly the Cold War itself. To address this perceived crisis, attention became focused in an unprecedented way on the nation's schools. In a significant shift of national political priorities, a new mission of schooling came into being. Schools were now charged with ensuring America's preparedness to meet whatever scientific and technological challenges might lie ahead. It was no longer seen as adequate for schools simply to concentrate on providing the education that would produce reasonably competent, literate, and well-rounded adults. A quite specific political agenda had moved to the fore.

This shift marked a substantive change in the relationship between the federal government and the schools. Characterized by calls for a general toughening of standards and more rigorous curricula (especially in mathematics and science), the reform movement that coalesced in the 1950s represented unprecedented federal involvement in the conduct of public schooling. By the middle of the following decade, other changes in America's schools and in their relationship to the federal government were under way as well. To the delight of many educators, public schools were tapped to serve as the centerpiece for President Johnson's Great Society program.

Johnson's predecessor in the White House, John F. Kennedy, had fought a spirited battle on behalf of increasing federal aid to public schools. But resistance arose out of concerns that this aid would open the floodgates for even more federal intervention as well. Kennedy also drew fire from Catholics who demanded that any such federal assistance be made available to parochial as well as public schools. This was a thorny issue in that it raised constitutional questions centering on the separation of church and state.

When Johnson became president, he was able, as part of a wider vision that became known as the Great Society program, to skirt many of these objections with a series of bills that provided aid to both parochial and private schools as well as to their public counterparts. His efforts culminated in the monumental 1965 Elementary and Secondary Education Act. Between 1964 and 1967, federal expenditures for education and technical training more than doubled, rising from $5 billion to $12 billion. Distribution of this aid was based on the economic circumstances of the students themselves, not just on the needs of particular schools. While many did benefit from Johnson's efforts, "as a mechanism to improve the quality of education in the ghettos and the nation's depressed rural backwaters, the education act was not a notable success," writes historian David Burner. "There was too little money, and inevitably it was spread too thin. It was also misspent. Little of it went into innovative programs; much was used to reduce the school-tax burden of local householders."[8] (This is not to say that the Great

Society program was across the board an unmitigated failure: far from it. For example, the 1960s saw the most significant decrease in poverty in the nation's history. At the dawn of the decade, more than 20 percent of the American people lived below the poverty line. By the end of the decade, that percentage had dropped to 12.)

Educational reform efforts in the 1960s were significantly influenced by two reports. The first of these, based on a study commissioned by the U.S. Department of Health, Education and Welfare and published in 1966, examined the causes of successes and failures among America's school children. Based on data gathered from a series of tests and questionnaires put together by sociologist James S. Coleman and his associates, it soon became known as the Coleman Report. Respondents included more than 645,000 students and some 20,000 teachers in more than 4,000 schools across the country. Computers and complex statistical procedures were used to process and analyze the massive amounts of data. All of this was accomplished in a mere two years. It was, by all accounts, an astonishing achievement and would later inform President Richard Nixon's education program.

The Coleman Report concluded, among other things, that a student's family and peers were likely to have a far greater impact on a student's performance in school than were such variables as teacher salaries, class sizes, and spending on school facilities.[9] Such findings found certain correlates in the Moynihan Report published in 1965.

The Moynihan Report, written by Daniel Patrick Moynihan when he was a Labor Department official in the Johnson administration, indicated that the higher rates of poverty found among black Americans were largely the result of broken homes and single-parent family structures.[10] Critics accused Moynihan of "either 'blaming the victim' or imposing white middle-class family values on a minority whose family structure was different but not necessarily inferior."[11] Writing a decade after the publication of Moynihan's *The Negro Family*, professor of psychology William

Ryan reported:

> The ten years that have elapsed since the publication of *The Negro Family* have demonstrated that its critics were quite correct in attacking Moynihan's inept and tendentious analysis of the data, graphs, and charts that were strewn so generously through his *Report*. His conclusions that the Negro family was "crumbling" were wrong, particularly his interpretation that the Black family was becoming more unstable in contrast to a stable white family that was "maintaining that stability." To put it most generously, his was simply a colossal misreading of the rather obvious changes that were taking place in the structure and function of the American family in general.[12]

But, Ryan notes, while

> Moynihan's critics appeared to win the battle—the subject of the Negro Family was stricken from the agenda of the 1966 White House Conference— . . . Moynihan clearly won the war. Subsequent articles, reviews and columns in *Life*, *Look*, *The New York Times* and other influential publications supported and adopted the Moynihan thesis and swamped the opposition, which by that point had grown to be a substantial group of critics, most of them trained social scientists.[13]

These reports influenced educational reform efforts in the 1960s by effectively releasing schools and those with authority over schools from their responsibility to serve all children well. After all, the reports concluded, inequities exist because of cultural differences, for which nothing can be done.

There were clearly political dimensions to the Sputnik-driven reform era of the mid-1960s. It nevertheless differed from eras to come in that the primary impetus for change remained within the educational establishment itself. Although the federal government played a major role, primarily by providing financial support and lending political weight, the actual changes in curriculum and pedagogy were still being designed and implemented by people connected with schools. There existed, in other words, a recipro-cal relationship between the two parties. This would change in the years to come as a new breed of reformer from outside the educa-tional system began simply to hand down mandates and, in some cases, turn them into law.

Even though the rhetoric of high expectations for all students declined in the latter half of the 1960s, thanks in part to the Coleman and Moynihan reports, the flow of philanthropic funding into certain educational coffers continued. Notable in this funding was an unprec-edented infusion of cash for research and development, as well as support for a variety of innovative and collaborative projects. As a result, in the years that followed, educators learned a great deal about contemporary approaches to schooling, learning, teaching, evaluat-ing, and how to implement change strategies. This was a bountiful harvest that held the promise of a phenomenal revitalizing of Amer-ican education, a promise that has yet to be fully realized.

Reform Part Two: The New School Order

In the aftermath of the 1960s, some reformers decided that it was the schools themselves that were failing and that the responsibili-ties for schooling should be assumed by people who for the most part were not educators. These repeated assertions gradually led to a shift in the public's perception of what schooling was or should be all about.

The late 1960s and early 1970s were difficult and tumultuous years as Vietnam, the Watergate scandal, the civil rights move-ment, women's liberation, the counterculture, and a host of other social upheavals rocked American society. Yet as chaotic as the 1960s were, it was nevertheless a decade of great hopes and high ideals as the peace and civil rights movements and strengthening our democratic values and infrastructure increasingly moved to center stage.

By the 1970s the nation's mood had undergone a dramatic shift. While there had been some success stories, most notably in the area of civil rights, there had been many disappointing failures as well. We had not effectively aligned our democracy with its rhetoric of equality and justice, and while we would enjoy a brief respite from major military engagements in the immediate wake of Vietnam, it would not be many years before we would once again be at war.

The 1970s, then, were for many a time of lowered expectations that included increasing disaffection with the schooling enterprise. Gone was the high level of exhilaration and optimism of the preceding decades. Interestingly, public support for the local school—not schooling—continued.

To try to address societal malaise and get America back on track, business and political leaders in particular called (once again) for a toughening of standards, accompanied by a longer school week and a longer school year. Greater emphasis, these reformers declared, should be placed on subjects such as history, mathematics, and the hard sciences. We needed to get "back to the basics," one more time. As an added incentive, teachers were no longer to be granted salary increases for time served or commitment to their profession. Instead, raises would be based on their success in raising students' test scores. The considerable amount of class time already being spent on test taking and preparation for it increased markedly.

This reform era differed from earlier ones in that it focused quite specifically on promoting the nation's economic and technological preeminence. Whereas in the past it had been thought that educated people were likely to be more productive and more creative and therefore a good general education would be a positive economic factor, schooling itself had not been viewed as an economic resource. The change was a momentous one. However, despite the economic interests driving this change, the reformers did not provide the kind of federal funding that Lyndon Johnson's initiatives had received. Instead, they pushed mandates on the local schools but fell short on providing the resources necessary to implement them.

This reform era also differed from its predecessors in that it took authority away from parents, educators, and local communities and placed it in the hands of government officials. Reflecting on this new relationship between the schools and government, Theodore Sizer writes, "Key policies are [now] often set and administered by bodies that are at a great distance from the communities [served] and highly unlikely, therefore, to be accountable to the particular people most affected by the quality of public education: the families of school-aged children." Sizer sees other problems with this new arrangement as well. "Leaders far from the schools can demand that high-quality work be done by the teachers and the students (say, in science)," he states, "without taking care that the conditions for that work—good laboratories, well-stocked libraries, appropriate student loads per teacher, adequate time—are available."[14]

As damaging to schools and the communities they served as this new breed of reformers was, it was only one part of the story. Other ideas had also begun to take root. By the late 1980s, a new loose-knit but widespread school improvement movement had emerged. Unlike the federal programs already firmly in place, this alternative movement approached educational change with a bottom-up (or grassroots) rather than a top-down strategy. Ideas such as site-based management were widely embraced for restructuring troubled schools.

Unlike existing federal initiatives, site-based management sought to move both the authority and the responsibility for decision making to the local level, where it would be placed in the hands of those most directly involved with and affected by what went on in the schools—principals, teachers, and parents. Conferences and in-service teacher education programs began to pay increasing attention to the school itself as a locus of change. Some state policymakers began to see the wisdom of this approach, and the push to "empower" educators at the local level was broadly championed. Philanthropic foundations soon joined in the effort.

University researchers interested in studying school change and innovation began to realize that funding their research might well depend, at least in part, on their willingness to collaborate with schools and school districts rather than work as outside observers.

These efforts were encouraging. For one thing, they enjoyed considerable support among both parents and educators. For another, they generally reflected the lessons gleaned from the many research efforts undertaken to examine schools and schooling in the late 1960s and early 1970s. They did not, however, receive the level of long-term financial and political support that would have been necessary to sustain them. Local schools simply did not gain the resources or political clout they needed to exercise their own renewal.

Reform and Its Many Problems

There are many reasons that school reform efforts fail. One is that they usually assume a much greater degree of uniformity on the part of schools, teachers, and students than actually exists or could ever exist in a nation as diverse as the United States. Students with differing cultural backgrounds come with many different personalities, interests, abilities, and so on. Their experiences and upbringing differ enormously. Their home and community environments differ. Their access to knowledge and opportunities to learn differ markedly.

Research makes clear that in the common third-grade classroom in the United States, the range of academic achievement spans more than three years from top to bottom. In a fourth-grade class, that range increases to more than four years. This pattern essentially repeats itself, increasing from one grade level to the next as student populations grow older. In fact, in a typical fourth-grade class at midterm, less than 15 percent of the students are likely to be at what is generally considered grade level in all subjects. Such variability, it was learned, is "reduced only moderately through so-called 'ability grouping.'"[15] Given such findings, a one-size-fits-all approach to school reform would seem to be quite inappropriate.

There are other problems with these recent reform movements. For one thing, a simple, standardized curriculum of reading, writing, and arithmetic cannot adequately prepare young people to participate as citizens in a democratic society. Democracy requires a particular kind of schooling, the apprenticeship in liberty referred to earlier. If schools are going to be effectual and relevant, and if they are to meet their moral obligations to a democratic public, they must have the prescience and flexibility to adapt independently to changes in their surroundings and in the specific populations they serve. Inflexible, prepackaged, homogenized approaches can serve only to stifle creativity and innovation and make it far more likely that whatever teaching does take place will be out of step with the greater social surround in which the school is embedded. "Educators must rethink what education is, what schools are for," we have argued, "and they must examine and rework the structures and practices that have always been out of sync for some students and are now revealed to be inappropriate to many."[16]

At the heart of this reworking of structures and practices is the change mechanism itself. Life, as most of us realize, is a continual process of change and adaptation. A single day rarely, if ever, turns out to have been what we had anticipated it would be. The science of ecology teaches us that organisms that do not adapt to changes in their surroundings are not long for this world. The rigidity of most reform agendas is anything but ecological—shackling the spirit and draining the lifeblood out of what ought to be a joyous and adventuresome exploration of human knowledge and understanding. Our schools do not need still another reform movement. They need to learn to incorporate, as an integral aspect of their day-to-day operations, a process of ongoing, systemic renewal.

To do this, educators and concerned others will need to adopt a more holistic view of the educational process. Instead of regarding schooling as consisting of a loosely choreographed series of essentially unconnected components or modules or classes wherein any one unit can be altered without affecting the whole, it will be far more useful to understand that schooling amounts to a good deal more than merely the sum total of its parts. The experience of schooling, and what is gleaned from that experience, provides far more than, say, what a geography class alone has to offer.

When we dive into a deep pool of cool water, for example, we do not experience "cool," or "wet," or "buoyancy" as a series of isolated events to be processed independently of one another. Rather, what we experience is a whole cumulative rush of sensations all swirled together and enveloping us at once. That rush of sensations is far greater and more complex than "cold" plus "wet" plus "buoyant." This is very much the way students experience school—indeed, it is the way all of us experience life. To make sense of school—or anything else in life—we seek patterns. We look for the "glue" that holds the whole together, that gives the experience meaning, purpose, direction. This is why schools routinely write mission statements. It is a way of saying, "This is our focus, this is what we are all about." Students will provide their own "glue" or their own narrative for schooling if they perceive that none exists. That narrative may be as simple as "mindless distraction" if the experience of schooling consists of nothing more than drifting from one classroom satellite to another. Or they may conclude that school is all about test taking if that is the dominant focus of the majority of their teachers. In other words, if we want the experience of schooling to have worthwhile meaning for those being schooled, then we must put that meaning there intentionally and explicitly.

To return to the pool for a moment, what do we do once we're in the water? If we have any presence of mind at all, we certainly don't behave as though nothing has changed (unless of course we're deliberately trying to drown). We start to swim. We start thinking about whether we need to get warm and dry. We start breathing differently. Our pulse accelerates. In other words, we adapt. Whether one is a student, a teacher, or an administrator, each day is more likely than not an inexorable process of adapting. Someone asks a question you never anticipated. A problem arises you hadn't foreseen. If we tie a person's wrists and ankles and throw him into the deep end of the pool, he is probably going to drown. Yet this is precisely what many reformers would, in effect, have us do to our schools. And when schools conform and start to flounder, as they commonly do, they have no choice but to look to the reformers for a lifeline because their ability to adapt has been lessened. One wonders: Wouldn't it make more sense to have them learn to "swim" on their own, and to free them to do so?

The Rhetoric of Reform and Renewal

The differences between renewal and reform are considerable. As Roger Soder explains, "embedded in both 'reform' and 'renewal' are basic views of the world, basic views of human nature, and basic views of the way individuals do business in this world. . . . A careful examination of the . . . rhetorical claims of reform and renewal will give readers a reasonably good sense of what is embedded in those claims."[17]

Rhetorically, the views expressed and the claims made by renewers and reformers can seem quite similar. In practice they are not. The differences are most evident in the ways in which each approach is actually implemented and in the pattern that emerged in our review of the history of recent reform movements. Both approaches claim to address issues such as social injustice, racism, and sexism. But, Soder notes, in the case of renewal, "justice, equity, diversity, access to knowledge, shared power, democracy, republican government, and so forth are often explicit issues to be worked on over the long haul."[18] In other words, they become part of a greater education narrative that transcends the purview of individual disciplines and unite to form a comprehensive, overarching mission for the entire enterprise of schooling. They are not add-ons or afterthoughts. They become a part of the recognizable pattern in which the educational experience is embedded.

Inherent in these contrasting approaches championed by reformers and renewers are fundamentally different ideas about human nature, particularly with respect to freedom. Soder juxtaposes the two perspectives this way: "We can accept the word of Dostoevsky's Grand Inquisitor. People don't want freedom, the

Grand Inquisitor reasons. They can't stand to have it, will do anything to get rid of it, and want to be ruled by miracle, mystery, and authority. Or we can argue that people want freedom and that freedom is an inherent part of the human condition. What do the rhetoric of reform and renewal say about freedom?"[19]

There are essentially two ways in which individuals can go about doing things: they can either be told what to do or they can determine their own goals and how they will try to achieve them. In the case of the former, the "prevailing but not necessarily 'right' and certainly not attractive view involves the exercise of force from those on high and the requirement of compliance from those below." This is more than just an authoritarian view of what constitutes a desirable power structure. As Soder suggests, it is also a particular view of humanity, of human potential, and of human freedoms. He then explains, "Compliance is never edifying, it never rings with human dignity, and it never pulses with excitement and curiosity and wonder. You'd never come running home from school telling your parents how much you complied that day and how much you liked it."[20] We have to ask ourselves, Is this the worldview that ought to be guiding the education of our young?

Oppressive tyranny demands compliance, whether that compliance is brought about by bribery or threat of force. But this is only one kind of tyranny. On a more subtle level, there is the tyranny of omission. Like oppressive tyranny, the tyranny of omission also demands compliance. "The tyranny of omission denies a hearing, denies consideration of things, denies voices," Soder explains. "When I attended the Seattle public schools in the 1950s, nobody gave much thought to intramural basketball for girls. The question of girls' basketball never even got to the table. It wasn't an issue. In a tyranny of omission, the unwelcome, the nontraditional, the threatening, the irritating, and the inconvenient are the songs that never make society's playlist."[21]

When we limit the scope of our knowledge, the depth and breadth of our understanding of ourselves and our fellow beings and the world around us, we limit options, we restrict potential, and we cripple imagination. What good is democracy if we do not have the intellectual tools and freedoms necessary to substantively exercise our rights, freedoms, and responsibilities as citizens? We cannot be expected to make wise, informed choices if we are not fully aware of the options and how to evaluate them. People have to be willing, able, and allowed to ask tough questions, to explore and to discover, to experiment, to challenge, to imagine, to create. Such ideas are not compatible with the language of compliance, and they rail against the tyranny of omission.

Reform movements, and the rhetoric that accompanies them, often omit what should be central to the educational experience. "The language of school reform," we have noted, "virtually eschews reference to the maturing of the self into greater wisdom, civility, civic-mindedness, democratic character, and participation in the whole of the human conversation." For reformers, "education is seen as an instrument rather than a value in its own right, the needs of the workforce outweigh human needs, and the sheer dourness and weight of the rhetoric of schooling hangs like a dark cloud over the lives of children."[22]

The tyranny of omission surfaces in the very language of reform. "The language of reform carries with it the traditional connotation of things gone wrong that need to be corrected, as with delinquent boys or girls incarcerated in reform schools. This language is not uplifting. It says little or nothing about the nature of education, the self, or the human community. Through sheer omission it dehumanizes. Prescriptions are given; corrective actions are to be taken by those identified as accountable (who are not the reformers but are those to be reformed)." The idea "is to bring all those recalcitrant entities out there into a linear, well-managed system—to align them in pursuit of common goals, methods, and outcomes."[23] One would have thought that in the several hundred years of public schooling in the United States of America we might have managed to come up with something a little more imaginative and uplifting.

Renewal offers a real alternative. It differs from reform in that the "language is multidimensional, relatively free of good guys/bad guys and (to the frustration of many reformers) of the linearity of specified ends, means, and outcomes. The language and the ethos of renewal have to do with the people in and around schools improving their practice and developing the collaborative mechanisms necessary to better their schools."[24] As Nel Noddings points out, the very "*idea* of renewal is different [from that of reform]. It attends to the underlying ideals and purposes of democratic education. It takes seriously the judgment of John Dewey that a democratic society 'must have a type of education which gives individuals a personal interest in social relationships and control, and the habits of mind which secure social changes without introducing disorder.'"[25] While reform is rooted in a remote, top-down authoritarian power structure, renewal is local, holistic, organic, and rooted in the communities it serves. It flies in the very face of the Grand Inquisitor's pronouncements of people preferring to be ruled by miracle, mystery, and authority.

What Is at Stake

The relationships among democracy, schooling, and educational renewal should not be taken lightly. They are interconnected in ways that, taken together, form a magnificent tapestry of human freedoms and dignity. Their sum is indeed far greater than the parts. Once we sacrifice any one thread, the entire fabric begins to unravel. Democracy is every bit as fragile and vulnerable as schooling is. Democracy's enemies know this every bit as much as democracy's proponents do. Walter Parker has spent many years examining the issues surrounding democracy and education. He reminds us that

> democracies are scarce and their incumbencies are brief. All of
> them, including the United States, are young, and most of them are
> only nominal democracies: representatives are elected by adults
> who vote, and whose votes count equally, and individuals have
> rights. Yet, it is not so much "we the people" who govern in these

fledgling democracies as it is power elites who govern. Ordinary citizens' civic competence goes undeveloped or, if nurtured to some extent somewhere along the line, atrophies through disuse. The consequence is the degradation of what Hannah Arendt called the public sphere.[26]

Others have expressed similar concerns. "Public education is an idea, not a mechanism," Theodore Sizer has written. "It promises every young citizen a fair grounding in the intellectual and civic tools necessary to have a decent life in this culture and economy. It promises the rest of us that the rising generations have the tools to keep America a place worthy of residence. It signals that we are one—*e pluribus unum.*"[27]

Linda Darling-Hammond has offered this assessment of the present state of our democratic work in progress: "Right now our democracy is in trouble," she states.

> Only about one-third of our citizens feel sufficiently interested or empowered to participate in a regular way in the political process. Racial, ethnic, and class divisions are growing as confusion about vast social changes creates a search for scapegoats. The ability of citizens to come together for positive social action in their local communities seems undermined by a combination of intergroup antagonism and a sense of cynicism and hopelessness about the usefulness of collective effort. Meanwhile, dramatically unequal access to education and employment routinely and systematically disadvantages low-income students and students of color and results in growing rates of crime, incarceration, structural unemployment, homelessness, drug use, and social dysfunction. These conditions increasingly victimize those trapped in a growing underclass, as well as all of those who pay—financially and socially—for its costs to the broader society. In many and growing ways, unequal access to the kind of education needed to sustain a democracy threatens the very foundations of our nation.[28]

The Agenda for Education in a Democracy we propose is more than an effort simply to revitalize a faltering civics curriculum. It is about restoring a shared humanity to the educational process. It is about the need to make caring, compassion, freedom, dignity, and responsibility central to the mission of schooling. It is about placing power and responsibility—concepts more demanding of the individual than is accountability—in the hands of those who need and deserve it. It is about taking the idea of excellence seriously. It is about taking democracy seriously. It is about having real faith in real people to do what is right, just, and honorable. It seems unconscionable to think that we might dare propose to do otherwise. Yet, in an address given on October 24, 2002, to the annual meeting of the National Network for Educational Renewal, one speaker, in words reminiscent of Al Haber's cited at the beginning of this chapter, observed that

> the prospects for the *Agenda's* educational narrative of developing democratic character in the young becoming at least a companion mission to the current economic mission of schooling appear to be less promising than they were a decade ago. The enormous nationwide community of educational organizations and agencies and its rhetoric of commitment to public schooling as the mainstay of our democracy remains virtually mute and hapless in the face of reform agendas and accompanying rhetoric moving us toward a privatized system of schooling. The ever-vigorous debate that once characterized this educational community and significantly influenced policy has been colonized by the federal government to a degree that threatens the democratic intent of the Constitution.[29]

Chapter Five

Democracy, Education, and the Human Conversation

Democracy is both demanding and inspiring. It is more than a lofty theoretical framework designed to settle arguments and resolve disputes. It is more than a set of ironclad criteria for countries to meet in order to become members of an international club. And as we've said before, it requires more of its citizens than voting at election time. When we look beyond the political trappings and historical lineage, we find that democracy is about who we are as individuals and how we live together as families, friends, neighbors, and citizens.

Too often we ignore the real substance of democracy—people—and focus on the idea and its institutional structures. If a country meets certain criteria (it has elected officials, an uncensored press, citizens' rights, and others) then it is a democracy, we say. We pay little attention, however, to how these criteria play out in reality. We rarely think to ask questions the answers to which might offer a comprehensive view of the state of democracy in a given nation. For example: Do we model civility and respect in our interactions with others? Do our communities readily welcome newcomers—even (and especially) those who may look different or speak differently? Do community leaders—such as teachers, parents, and shopkeepers—make it clear that racism, sexism, bigotry, and homophobia hold no value? Is the welfare of others a concern shared by all? Do we ensure that all of our fellow citizens have access to adequate food, health care, housing, and education? Do the elected officials genuinely represent the citizens who elect them? Do the majority of citizens vote? Do citizens participate in the decision-making processes that govern them? Do officials actually work to carry out the wishes of the people? Do the media report freely, independently, and critically on the affairs of the state? Do the media take seriously their responsibility to inform the public about issues that affect their lives? Do all citizens enjoy equally the same rights and privileges, or are those rights applied differently to different groups on the basis of race, economic status, class, gender, sexual preference, political affiliation, and so on? How do citizens regard one another and their political representatives? Are important issues routinely subject to serious, open, public debate that includes a full range of relevant ideas and opinions? Do political leaders look up to their constituents, or down on them? Is public education widely supported, highly valued, well funded, and recognized for the essential contribution it makes to a democratic public? Is the democratic mission of schooling understood and taken seriously by the public at large?

This list of questions could be a good deal longer. Though far from exhaustive, it does, however, make the point that to think of democracy as merely a political system in which people get to vote once in a while is to miss entirely the very essence of what democracy is all about. Democracy, first and foremost, is a shared way of life. It begins with who we are as individuals and the relationships we have with those around us, and it radiates outward from that center to encompass all of humanity. Democracy does not and cannot abruptly stop at county, state, or national political borders, because it is, in essence, about human relationships, and human relationships do not adhere to strict political boundaries any more than they stick to boundaries of race, sex, religion, class, economic status, or some other prejudicial criterion.

When we look at democracy in this way, we begin to see why schools in democratic societies are different from schools in other societies. Although all schools strive to produce literate, socially and vocationally competent people, in a democracy schools must also enculturate the young into a unique social and political environment—the idea being to develop in individuals what we call "democratic character." The reason for this is, "[t]here must be conditions in place for democracy to be created, sustained, recovered, and improved. People create conditions. People must have a given set of dispositions or characteristics that will most likely lead to the creation of those conditions."[1]

Soder emphasizes the role of schools in developing democratic character. "These dispositions or characteristics are taught and reinforced in homes, churches, private associations, street corners—and schools. I continue to believe that it is to the schools that we must look for sustained attention to the development of the character of a democratic people."[2]

Education: It's Everywhere

Democracy recognizes that even though a population may be unified by citizenship or even agreement on certain principles and ideals, it can and should still harbor great diversity. In a democracy it is essential that the majority not ignore the beliefs and concerns of minorities. It is also essential that powerful minorities not exclude the views of those with whom they disagree or impose their will on others.

This is not to argue that all views and beliefs carry equal weight or validity, or that any belief—no matter how extreme—is acceptable. Some beliefs, as history amply demonstrates, are so clearly hostile to the welfare of others or harmful to the community as a whole—such as those held by racists, homophobes, and religious fanatics, to name but a few—that they simply have no place in a society that regards itself as just or democratic. Thus, one of the most important responsibilities of educators in a democracy is to enable youngsters to differentiate between constructive and destructive views and beliefs. In this sense, democracy education prepares individuals to make decisions and choices that benefit not only the self, but the community as well. To do this students must acquire a degree of what might best be called *wisdom* on their journey to selfhood. As John Goodlad explains,

> The lesson that comes through to me in the drama of humankind's struggle for individual liberty in a free society pertains to the centrality of the mind. Whether authority be derived from cruel tyrant or seemingly benign guru, power lies in numbing the individual mind in favor of groupthink. The full development of selfhood is sacrificed to an imposed common good that smoothes out deviations. We cringe over the brutalities routinely administrated to deviants in a tyrannical régime. We are appalled over the lives lost when still another fanatical cult self-destructs. But we are incredibly complacent about—indeed, often serenely untouched by—the millions of selfhoods left adrift in contexts that deny or thwart their fulfillment. Education is so ubiquitous that we fail to comprehend its power and see the consequences of its denial, misuse, and abuse until we are on the verge of and in crisis.[3]

Education is a universal given. It exists everywhere and, if not all the time, much of the time. In fact, education is, whether we like it or not, inescapable. That fact, in and of itself, is neither good nor bad. Education is, as we have said in Chapter One, value-neutral in that it can be positive, put to constructive ends, made useful or otherwise good; or it can be negative and of a destructive nature. In some extreme cases, education can actually be extremely dangerous. One can easily learn or teach another person how to build a bomb, for example.

We are all students, of a sort, most of the time. For most of us, the older we get the better we distinguish between good education and bad education. When we are young, of course, we are most vulnerable to education of all sorts. And much of it we don't even recognize as being "educative." The education that schools strive to deliver is really a comparatively small part of a much bigger picture. Consider, for example, the prevalence of a certain kind of ubiquitous education delivered by the mass media. Todd Gitlin writes,

> The place of media in the lives of children is worth special attention—not simply because children are uniquely impression-able but because their experience shapes everyone's future; if we today take a media-soaked environment for granted, surely one rea-son is that we grew up in it and can no longer see how remarkable it is. To illustrate the point, here are some findings from a national survey of media conditions among American children aged two through eighteen. The average American child lives in a household with 2.9 televisions, 1.8 VCRs, 3.1 radios, 2.6 tape players, 2.1 CD players, 1.4 video game players, and 1 computer. Ninety-nine per-cent of these children live in homes with one or more TVs, 97 percent with a VCR, 97 percent with a radio, 94 percent with a tape player, 90 percent with a CD player, 70 percent with a video game player, 69 percent with a computer. Eighty-eight percent live in homes with two or more TVs, 60 percent in homes with three or more. Of the 99 percent with a TV, 74 percent have cable or satellite service. . . .
>
> The uniformity of this picture is no less astounding. A great deal about the lives of children depends on their race, sex, and social class, but access to major media does not. For TV, VCR, and radio ownership, rates do not vary significantly among white, black, and Hispanic children, or between girls and boys. For television and radio, rates do not vary significantly according to the income of the community.
>
> How accessible, then, is the media cavalcade at home? Of chil-dren eight to eighteen, 65 percent have a TV in their bedrooms, 86 percent a radio, 81 percent a tape player, 75 percent a CD player. Boys and girls are not significantly different in possessing this bounty, though the relative usages do vary by medium. Researchers also asked children whether the television was "on in their homes even if no one is watching 'most of the time,' 'some of the time,' 'a little of the time,' or 'never.'" Homes in which television is on "most

of the time" are termed *constant television households*. By this measure, 42 percent of all American households with children are constant television households.[4]

All of these percentages would likely be higher today.

Television basically has two messages to deliver and it delivers those messages relentlessly: one, you, the viewer, are the most important person out there in television land; and two, *buy something*. These are not the kinds of messages on which great civilizations are or have ever been built. They do not do anything to cultivate our sense of being actors, as opposed to spectators, in a democratic society. Nor do they fill our hearts with hope, nurture the soul, or inspire us to imagine a brighter, more harmonious, more just future. Instead, they do little but breed a faintly smug and self-righteous complacency, a grim cynicism, and a treadmill addiction to instant gratification through compulsive, habitual consumption. Human beings need and deserve better.

Schools, no matter how good and committed they are to doing what they do, no matter how well-trained and competent their teachers, cannot counteract the influence of parents, peers, media, and all that constitutes the social surround. Nor should they. But they do have a responsibility to open young eyes to things that might otherwise never be encountered. We can and must ask that our schools provide some basic and useful knowledge, that they try to cultivate good habits of the heart and mind, and that they equip the young, to the best of their ability, to enter an unknowable future. These expectations may sound simple, but they are formidable challenges, as any parent can attest. Fortunately, public schools, by their very nature and by virtue of their "publicness," are in a unique position to accomplish these goals.

Knowledge, Wisdom, and Quality Education

In some ways, the public school resembles a scaled-down version of society itself. School is a society—of sorts—within a society. It has many of the same virtues and many of the same problems that the larger society has. Social and economic problems that exist in a community are likely to be manifest in that community's schools. School bureaucracies often resemble the bureaucracies of local governments. In this sense, and many others, the walls of the classroom are quite porous. Schools are not the sanctuaries we'd like to think they are. For just these reasons, schools are where most of us learn to navigate the world outside the home. It is where we are first formally introduced to what we might call *the human conversation*.

If we are going to live in a society made up of many races and religions, ancestries and belief systems, it only makes sense that the classrooms that are supposed to prepare us to participate meaningfully in such a society should reflect a similar diversity. After all, we don't teach children how to swim without allowing them to get wet. We don't learn to repair a bicycle by imagining what it might be like to do so. A classroom that prepares students for democracy, therefore, is going to be a classroom that not only welcomes but values and thrives on the kind of diversity on which a healthy democracy also thrives.

Diversity is not limited solely to the makeup of the student body. Diverse views, ideas, opinions, and theories must also be a part of a democracy curriculum. Our society is not of one mind, sharing a uniform view of the world. Humankind's best ideas have often been amalgams of several competing views. Justice does not live at the extremities, but in the messy uncertainties and ambiguities that occupy the center. Peaceful resolution is found in persuasion and compromise, not in brute force or in mandates handed down by extremists and fanatics. So it not only makes sense but is essential to the health of the human community that youngsters learn to value intellectual as well as social diversity.

This means that as part of our apprenticeship to liberty we must learn to listen to and understand the views of others, and to appreciate the values inherent in those views—even if, in the end, we may disagree with them.

It also means that students must learn to distinguish what are and are not useful, relevant data and legitimate, logical arguments. We all start out in life adopting the views of others whom we admire, respect, or love. But these are views we parrot. They are not and cannot be our own views until we have taken the step of critically examining them, their origins and implications, the soundness of their reasoning, and their moral correctness. A democracy curriculum ought to help us learn how to do this. As Nel Noddings points out, "a liberal democracy depends for its legitimacy on the continuing and voluntary affirmation of a critical citizenry. This means . . . that students must be encouraged to inquire, to object, to think critically."[5] Teachers and students alike must learn to ask the difficult questions, the questions that make us uneasy, the questions that have no comfortable, pat answers.

Education that eschews this responsibility is of little, if any, value. "It has been the premise of all pedagogy since Socrates," Benjamin Barber notes, "that the answer that cannot withstand questioning is not worth much, just as the story that cannot withstand challenge is without value to liberty. Our cognitive discomfort in the face of uncertainty disposes us to impose cloture on criticism and questioning. But the quest for learning that defines the classroom needs to resist 'the quest for certainty.'"[6] We would do well to remember that if scientists were certain about their understanding of the world around them, there would be no scientific advancement, and hence no science. Science is based on *uncertainty*, not certainty. Most of what scientists have ever thought to be true has, in time, proven not to be. It makes much more sense for youngsters to learn how to ask questions and search for answers than it does to "teach" them what science "knows." The same is true, for example, of morality. Morals that are "carved in stone" are not morals at all. They are dogma, which invite no moral judgment. Moral progress is not possible without thoughtful reflection and critical examination, both of which require careful training and nurturing.[7]

Patriotism provides another example of the difference between schooling as it is shaped by democracy and schooling in countries that are not democratic and wherein patriotism is often little more than flag waving and blind obedience to authority. Saluting the flag and reciting the Pledge of Allegiance are, in and of themselves, not proof of either patriotism or democratic character. Unexamined patriotism is not patriotism at all. It is, rather, nationalism, and that often has proved to be dangerous. Nationalism is much more the breeding ground of dictators, imperialists, and tyrants than is democracy. If we understand patriotism to be *the love of one's country*, then we must remember that love is not something we feel because we have been told to feel it or because it has been drilled into us. Love is something that must develop over time. It comes from intimate acquaintance with the object of our affection. That object need not and cannot be without flaws. If love required that we see only perfection, it would be as elusive as perfection itself.

To know a country is to know its story, warts and all. If people are to develop the love of country we call patriotism, there must be a narrative, a story that they can feel part of. That narrative, that history, must be a comprehensive one, told with candor and courage. It must be able to withstand the harsh light of historical scrutiny. "The American story that cannot withstand sharp interrogation is worthless," Barber writes.

> If we fear that subjecting American ideals to such questioning may undermine them, then these ideals are far too frail. If we believe that querying the legitimacy of some particular appeal to universality (the claim that white male property holders in 1787 embodied "We the People," for example) may erode the very notion of universalism, then we impeach genuine universalism by assuming it cannot be distinguished from its counterfeits. If we think that to impose claims of impartiality to criticism may breed nihilist relativism, then we end up supporting not impartiality but the hegemony of whichever elite has managed to lay claim to it.[8]

The wisdom that we all acquire over the course of what is often regarded as our "formative years," has to come from somewhere. What that wisdom consists of and where it comes from is of great importance. For not only does it ultimately define who we are as individuals, but it also helps foster the transcendence of the self that embeds each and every one of us in a community. That is why a democracy needs public schools: to help create a viable, robust, democratic public. If we care about having such a public, then we must care enough to ensure that we have the kinds of schools that will help to produce it. This is why schooling in a democracy bears a very special moral burden. As we have stated elsewhere,

> since wisdom has to do with the kinds of choices we make, wisdom is a moral concept. Education, then, is a moral undertaking. Consequently, teaching that seeks to go beyond the simplest rote learning is a moral endeavor.
>
> This is a frightening idea for many people, particularly those suffering psychological stress and experiencing fear because of their own loss of or failure to gain a secure sense of place in humankind. If, in fear, we hobble the schools in the development of wisdom in their students, we might as well close them and permit instruction to go on unrestrained by the controls we can properly place on our schools and teachers. Teaching the young is an incredibly risk-laden responsibility. We must be sure that a large part of it is done by wise, caring parents who understand the nature of education and by teachers who have experienced the best in liberal and professional studies in universities and in the exemplary schools with which such institutions must be in partnership.[9]

Fairness, Equity, and "Granfalloons"

Ours is a nation too often seen as dedicated to the pursuit of individual affluence. Accompanying this pursuit is a callous indifference to the poverty and suffering of others. Quality and excellence have little place in the kingdom of cold, hard cash as we wage unrelenting economic warfare on one and all. We have created a monstrous gap between the haves and have-nots that is both economic and political. The voices of the vast majority of

Americans have been virtually silenced. As one writer put it, even the "liberal movement in the United States of America, directed to equality in all realms of human endeavor, stumble[s] over the inflammatory issue of the distribution of wealth."[10] Yet ours is a nation that boasts of having gained the moral high ground with respect to fairness and equity.

This situation cannot help but have a significant impact on our schools. As we have already stated, schools are indelibly linked to the communities in which they reside. They do not and cannot exist separately from the community, and they cannot help but mirror the values and norms of the community. Unfairness and inequity in communities affect schools just as they do housing, businesses, employment opportunities, political leverage, lifestyle, and almost everything else. "Neither the public purpose nor the educative power of schools," Goodlad points out, "will be in good health until the educational capital of the surrounding context is raised significantly." He continues, noting that

> the notion of school reform as a tide raising the level of all boats is today both wrongheaded and mischievous. Wrong-headed because . . . even reform intended to help the disadvantaged helps the advantaged first. Mischievous because the dominance of private purpose in politically driven school reform of the past decade or so is not even directed to the impoverished and most needful. In effect, the concept that gave birth to and sustained a public system of schooling to ensure for all access to the knowledge and skills required for parenthood, work, citizenship, and personal comfort has been seriously eroded. Many people today, in contrast to those citizens who once connected such a system with both their own and the common good, are now devoted to the private cause of how to control and manipulate it for their own ends solely.[11]

Issues of unfairness and inequity are not limited to the economic sphere. Power, whether it be political, cultural, or

ideological, goes hand in hand with our economic disparity. As
Barber writes,

> The missing term in most recent arguments on behalf of neutrality,
> impartiality, and balance is power. . . . Power skews theoretical neu-
> trality and unbalances apparently symmetrical relationships. There
> is no symmetry between the homeless vagrant who shuns the rich
> and the rich pedestrian who shuns the homeless. The repellent slo-
> gans "Off the pigs!" and "Kill the niggers!" are equally appalling
> expressions of hatred and intolerance, but while the antiestablish-
> ment rhetoric reflects a desperate escalation by the powerless, the
> establishment's own resort to polemic is a quite deadly reflection of
> actual kill ratios in most of the race riots that have occurred in real
> American cities in real American history. . . . In the classroom, this
> means that a teacher cannot necessarily treat as equals powerful and
> embedded systems of thought and radical challenges to them. For
> example, the story of the American Frontier seen from the Sioux
> perspective may get a little extra help from the teacher who is satis-
> fied that students are already sufficiently familiar with more conven-
> tional perspectives.[12]

It is not possible to create a wise and thoughtful public if, as
educators, we fail to grapple with the complicated, difficult, and
messy issues that human beings have confronted since the dawn of
civilization. It is a terrible failing for a teacher to avoid (or worse,
be required to avoid) discussing a topic simply because *it is too
controversial*. It is also dangerous. A pristine, sanitized, mytholo-
gized fantasy world is the stuff of amusement parks. It is pleasant,
nonthreatening, entertaining. It is designed to help us forget the
real world. It is not designed to help us better understand the real
world, or to try to find solutions to untidy problems, or to live richer
and more rewarding lives, or to promote justice and equity, or to
strengthen communities, or to make us wise. Because it is rooted
deeply and inextricably in the troublesome and tumultuous world
that real people actually inhabit, real and meaningful learning is

never easy. It is not always pleasant, neat, or comfortable. And there is good reason that it must not be allowed to be so.

Most of us grew up with a stifling sense of political insignificance. By and large, we are not very well equipped for meaningful engagement in the affairs of the communities in which we live. Few of us even have the time, the inclination, or the energy for such activity. A majority of us in this country feel so disenfranchised that we don't even bother to vote. History too often presents the past as a series of stories or chapters, each with seemingly superhuman heroes and villains, characters much bigger and far more significant than we are. Most of our ancestors show up as nameless members of some vast but seemingly ineffectual sea of humanity, a sort of backdrop of faceless victors and victims before which the great dramas of the past are acted out by a royal cast of brilliant and distinguished actors, and most of them adorned with all the trappings of wealth and power. Motion pictures and television reinforce this sense of the impotence and diminished stature of "the common people," who are not and probably never will be stars or heroes or politicians or generals or CEOs. Every once in a while a Rosa Parks or a Cesar Chavez or a Ralph Nader surfaces, but soon they too are catapulted into the spotlight, and once again many of us are left believing that the real doers and shakers in this world are made of something quite different from the rest of us.

Democracy demands that we strip away the masks of the faceless so they may be counted among the living, that we give names to the nameless, and that the voices to whom those names belong have a chance not just to be heard but also to be listened to. Democracy is based on the idea that we all can and should share in steering the course of our lives; that we are each of us, to some degree, leaders in our own right; that we each have a voice and that every voice counts; that silence and servility are not the stuff of which vibrant, self-governing communities are made. When a teacher fails to take seriously issues such as equity and fairness, fails to delve into their history, fails to grapple with their problems and complexities, that teacher in effect helps ensure their perpetuity by numbing or neutralizing the very voices that might possibly demand and offer solutions. To omit that which we find unflattering or distasteful from our history is not only to distort the past, but also to help blind us to the present.

We often hear in the press and on television that our government is taking this or that action on behalf of the "national interest." This national interest suggests that somehow all of us—the rich, the poor, and the middle class—share a common set of concerns and goals. In truth, most of the time the national interest is little more than a euphemism for a very small, very wealthy, and very powerful group of elites who have little if anything in common with the vast majority of their countrymen and women. But if, as citizens, we have been disarmed by a failure on the part of our teachers to equip us to examine critically the world in which we live, then we are unlikely to ask the kinds of questions that we ought to be asking, or to seek the answers we ought to be seeking. Critical examination of the world around us is necessary if we are to develop sound, informed opinions about whether what is being done in our name is in fact in our best interests or not. If we have not been prepared to conduct even this most basic and essential inquiry, then we can hardly be said to have been prepared to make reasonable, let alone wise, decisions concerning our own collective governance.

Consider, for example, the state of the nation's economy, which is often described in broad, universal terms as though it had the same meaning and relevance to all of us. As historian Howard Zinn points out, "When the president declares happily that 'our economy is sound,' he will not acknowledge that it is not at all sound for 40 or 50 million people who are struggling to survive, although it may be moderately sound for many in the middle class, and extremely sound for the richest one percent of the nation who own 40 percent of the nation's wealth." [13]

Zinn recalls that novelist Kurt Vonnegut once came up with the term "'granfalloon' to describe a great bubble that must be punctured to see the complexity inside." [14] Education in support of democracy must deflate our "granfalloons"; it must dare to peer behind the curtain in the Magical Kingdom of Oz; it must enable us to see ourselves not only as we wish we were, but as we truly are. Otherwise, "education" is little more than a charade promoting complacency, servility, and ultimately the very kind of neglect that perpetuates social, economic, and political decay. When we go to Disneyland, we do so as spectators, as observers, as tourists. The action belongs to Goofy and Mickey Mouse, and to other actors. But when we leave Disneyland, we can no longer afford the luxury of being mere tourists in our own lives or spectators observing the lives of others. Luxury of that kind is simply too dangerous.

Introduction to the Human Conversation

Those who call attention to the imbalances and injustices inflicted by the powerful upon the powerless are often chastised and marginalized for being "politically correct" or too "multicultural." The assumption is made that their goal is to fragment and distort the "truth." There is a belief, harbored by some, that there exists somewhere such a thing as a body of "objective knowledge" and a "correct" view of the world that will be destroyed if others, especially those with less adulatory views, are allowed to enter the conversation. Those who fear such an outcome have good reason to, for there is no absolute objective knowledge any more than there is a single correct view of the world. All knowledge is, to some extent, fragmentary and subjective, and no one worldview deserves unmitigated universal acceptance. If it did, the human conversation itself would fall silent.

This is not to suggest that the human conversation is a search for some universal truth or grand consensus. But it does involve the ever-present search for narratives that lend meaning to who we are and what we're about. Neil Postman discusses narrative in *Building a Bridge to the Eighteenth Century*. He writes:

> I mean by "narrative" a story. But not any kind of story. I refer to *big* stories—stories that are sufficiently profound and complex to offer explanations of the origins and future of a people; stories that

construct ideals, prescribe rules of conduct, specify sources of authority, and, in doing all this, provide a sense of continuity and purpose. Joseph Campbell and Rollo May, among others, called such stories "myths." Marx had such stories in mind in referring to "ideologies." And Freud called them "illusions." No matter. What is important about narratives is that human beings cannot live without them. We are burdened with a kind of consciousness that insists on our having a purpose. Purposefulness requires a moral context, and moral context is what I mean by a narrative. The construction of narratives is, therefore, a major business of our species; certainly no group of humans has ever been found that did not have a story that defined for them how they ought to behave and why. That is the reason why there is nothing more disconcerting, to put it mildly, than to have one's story mocked, contradicted, refuted, held in contempt, or made to appear trivial. To do so is to rob a people of their reason for being. And that is why no one loves a story-buster, at least not until a new story can be found.[15]

Given the enormous diversity of the human population, to the extent that such agreement on certain major narratives is possible, such agreement has been largely reached. Around the world, for instance, most people feel that life is precious and has value in its own right, that good health is important and desirable, that suffering ought to be minimized to as great an extent as possible, that there is value in education, that love is a wonderful and universal human emotion, and so on. In other words, human beings everywhere already share a vast catalog of beliefs, emotions, perceptions, and understandings about the world we share. This commonality creates the necessary condition for the human conversation.

The substance of the human conversation centers not just on our commonalities but on what is unknown and what is contested. For example, we might wonder: Is there a reason we are here? Need existence have a reason? What constitutes a good life? What is just and what is not? What are morals? How do they work? How do they change? What is the relationship of past to present? Why *do* jackrabbits insist on crossing busy highways? (Not all topics in the human conversation are necessarily of a profound nature.) The reason that human beings, for generation after generation, persist in asking these kinds of questions is not that there is a widespread belief that decisive answers are to be found somewhere, somehow. It is because there is value in simply asking the questions and in the shared pursuit of their ever-elusive "answers." Because in that pursuit we pick up clues, we stumble across ideas, we encounter unanticipated arguments that shed light on our own existence, that give meaning anew to the world we inhabit, that turn our lives in directions that we find more rewarding, more fulfilling, more comforting and secure, or perhaps more complex than that which we had had before. We may never live The Good Life, but we can always get a little closer to living a good life. And therein is the essence and necessity of the human conversation. It is hard to imagine a general education worthy of the name that somehow fails to introduce the young to this conversation. It is universal.

Creating a Wise and Thoughtful Public

In recent years there has been a widely held perception that if we equip ourselves with enough television channels to watch and radio stations to listen to, and if we get every home, business, and classroom hooked up to the Internet, we will somehow strengthen our democracy while simultaneously elevating our collective intellect to that of utter genius. We have, until now, the thinking goes, been sorely lacking an adequate supply of information. This lack has in turn crippled us intellectually and resulted in our too often making poor decisions and erroneous calculations of all sorts. Happily, with the arrival of the digital age, the problem has at long last been solved. Or has it? Neil Postman summarizes our current state of affairs by suggesting that

> [t]he problem addressed in the nineteenth century was how to get more information to more people, faster, and in more diverse forms. For 150 years, humanity has worked with stunning ingenuity to solve this problem. The good news is that we have. The bad news is that,

in solving it, we have created another problem, never before experienced: information glut, information as garbage, information divorced from purpose and even meaning. As a consequence, there prevails among us what Langdon Winner calls "mythinformation"—no lisp intended. It is an almost religious conviction that at the root of our difficulties—social, political, ecological, psychological—is the fact that we do not have enough information. This, in spite of everyone's having access to books, newspapers, magazines, radios, television, movies, photographs, videos, CDs, billboards, telephones, junk mail, and, recently, the Internet. If I have left out some source of information, you can supply it. The point is that having successfully solved the problem of moving information continuously, rapidly, and in diverse forms, we do not know, for the most part, what to do with it or about it except to continue into the twenty-first century trying to solve a nineteenth-century problem that has already been solved. This is sheer foolishness, as any eighteenth-century savant would surely tell us. If there are people starving in the world—and there are—it is not caused by insufficient information. If crime is rampant in the streets, it is not caused by insufficient information. If children are abused and wives are battered, that has nothing to do with insufficient information. If our schools are not working and democratic principles are losing their force, that too has nothing to do with insufficient information. If we are plagued by such problems, it is because something else is missing.[16]

All the technological wizardry and all the data banks in the world are not going to miraculously create a wise and thoughtful public or, as we are learning, solve even many of the most basic human problems—such as hunger, poverty, illiteracy, and hate. It is easy, although usually rather costly, to provide ourselves with ever more data or to acquire more and more colorful technologies. It is not as quick or easy to do the real work of educating human beings for a better, more just, more democratic world. That requires the dedicated efforts of many skilled, conscientious, and motivated professionals. And most people already know and want this. When asked if they could change just one thing about American education, what would it be, time and again audiences across the country have overwhelming responded that they would see to it that every classroom had in it a well-trained, competent, caring teacher.

When we think in terms of what it takes to create a wise and thoughtful public, gardening easily lends itself as a useful metaphor. For democracy to thrive it needs rich soil to nurture it, deep roots to provide it with nutrients, and the strength to resist battering winds and the inevitable forces of erosion. Like the rich soil of a well-cared for garden, the fertile soil of democracy is made up of many diverse elements. Schools are only one component, but they are an important and necessary component.

In the previous chapter we briefly looked at the last fifty years of American education and at the reform movements, broadly speaking, that characterized those years. While much attention was paid during that time to curriculum content (more math, more science, more reading, writing, and computing), a remarkable dearth of attention was paid to development of what we have elsewhere termed *democratic character*—the dispositions and habits of heart and intellect that go into making caring, competent citizens. It is perhaps something more than coincidence that this neglect is reflected in our communities at large.

In *Bowling Alone*, his study of community in America, Robert D. Putnam summarizes recent trends in political participation this way:

On the positive side of the ledger, Americans today score about as well on a civics test as our parents and grandparents did, though our self-congratulation should be restrained, since we have on average four more years of formal schooling than they had. Moreover, at election time we are no less likely than they were to talk politics or express interest in the campaign. On the other hand, since the mid-1960s, the weight of the evidence suggests, despite the rapid rise in levels of education, Americans have become perhaps 10–15 percent less likely to voice our views publicly by running for office or writing Congress or the local newspaper, 15–20 percent less interested in politics and public affairs, roughly 25 percent less likely to vote, roughly 35 percent less likely to attend public meetings, both partisan and nonpartisan, and roughly 40 percent less engaged in party politics and indeed in political and civic organizations of all sorts. We remain, in short, reasonably well-informed spectators of public affairs, but many fewer of us actually partake in the game.[17]

Were we to try to explain our predicament in as few words as possible, we might say something to the effect that *we know a great deal, we just don't know what to do with what we know or what any of it really means.* We have spent enormously to ensure that we have access to all the newest facts and all the latest photographs and the most up-to-date databanks, but we have invested much less in developing the habits of inquiry and reflection that make all of that information useful. This is the difficult and challenging work of teachers. As Deborah Meier explains,

> The habits conducive to free inquiry don't just happen with age and maturity. They take root slowly. And uncertainties, multiple viewpoints, the use of independent judgment, and pleasure in imaginative play aren't luxuries to be grafted on to the mind-set of a mature scholar, suited only to the gifted few, or offered after school on a voluntary basis to the children of parents inclined this way. It's my contention that these are the required habits of a sound citizenry, habits that take time and practice.[18]

Schools alone cannot create or guarantee a wise and thoughtful public that is conscious of being part of the human conversation and thus prepared to create, sustain, and effectively participate in a democracy. Many elements must come together to do such work. But schools can provide the soil of democracy with a large portion of the nutrients it needs. Schools are where, with the right care and nurturing, the habits of democracy take root and begin to grow, where the young become aware of the human conversation in all of its glorious diversity and begin to participate in it.

Chapter Six

Renewal

It may be a good thing that most school innovations are cosmetic and don't last. Experienced teachers know that by itself a new text or a new approach to lesson planning or a newly mandated test will probably not lead to their students' increased engagement with knowledge and ideas. Teachers of the past several reform-laden decades have learned that the most recent Miracle Cure will soon be grist for tomorrow's skepticism (both their own and the public's) and for jokes targeted at schools and teachers. "If the latest change makes intuitive sense, fine," many say. "If not, be patient and it too will eventually fade away."

Teachers have also learned that even when they embrace these mandated fixes, the gains—if they occur—are usually short-lived. The enthusiasm and attention that accompany "the new" may bring short-term results, but once the newness fades, enthusiasm and attention fade as well. This phenomenon is similar to the Hawthorne Effect in experimental research, which explains short-term changes in behavior as due to the attention that research participants receive rather than to the power of the intervention itself.

Within a short time, "school reform" often looks a lot like what was happening before the reform.[1] In fact, reform—an externally driven something "new" replacing (at least temporarily) something thought to be "old"—is the antithesis of renewal—the primary change strategy embedded in the Agenda for Education in a Democracy.

Renewal as a Concept

Things left uncared-for tend to deteriorate. This year's crack in the cement welcomes next year's weeds. Peeling paint invites moisture and rot. The almost invisible leak in a pipe eventually destroys the floorboard. The tree root grown too big makes its way into the sewer line.

Minimal attention may ward off the worst decay. But minimal attention usually has minimal effect. A once-beautiful garden will quickly begin to break down if it is given only occasional water and a little weeding. But most of us generally don't pull up stakes and move simply because the paint on the windowsill starts to peel. And we don't destroy our old garden and start over from scratch each time the blooms begin to fade. The consumptionist tendency to discard the old in favor of the new doesn't help us much in such matters. We usually do better when we exercise patient, ongoing care and, while monitoring the effectiveness of that care, make adjustments where necessary. Such an approach, when applied to schooling, is what we call *educational renewal*.

Educational renewal is primarily designed to do two things. First, it is designed generally to prevent present conditions from deteriorating and to address problems that arise. But because schools are not yet—nor are they likely ever to be—good enough simply to maintain, renewal is, second, designed to make it possible to effect changes and to sustain those changes that prove desirable.

In Chapter Four we discussed the primarily rhetorical differences between educational reform and educational renewal. There are also profound differences in strategies and processes. Reforms generally come from external sources. They are usually mandated. They are thought to provide a comprehensive answer or solution. They are usually designed to replace rather than to fix something. Reformers tend to believe that an expert, rather than a practitioner, is required to solve problems; that solutions are context-independent—that is, that they will work in any school with any teacher at any time and with any group of students. Reformers often feel that those who are to implement reforms need not understand such things as the theory behind the reform; they just need to do as they're told.

We cited in Chapter Four Roger Soder's concept of renewal as a way of being rather than a received program or set of instructions to be implemented. Renewal efforts encompass an entire setting, such as a school, instead of simply targeting this or that component. Renewal does not affect only a few individuals; it involves everyone with responsibility for the setting's well-being. Renewal requires discussing and sharing information with others. In fact, observation and reflection are essential activities in the renewal process.[2]

Just as reformers make certain assumptions about how to address problems, those engaged in the practice of educational renewal have their own assumptions. For example, they assume that practitioners—that is, those actually working in the schools— have the capacity (or can acquire the capacity) to analyze problems, plan strategies for addressing those problems, and evaluate the impact of their efforts. They believe that context has meaning and must be considered when planning change strategies. For instance, a problem shared by two different schools may require quite different solutions if one of those schools happens to be in a rural Tennessee mountain town and the other is in an urban center in California. "Renewers" know that real progress and improvement take time and care.

In schools where renewal is effective, the staff—teachers, administrators, custodians, secretaries, bus drivers, and so on— come to view their school as a web of interconnected elements. They learn to recognize what is working and what isn't. They don't just focus on their own contributions; they look at the whole of the schooling experience. Their observations are shared with colleagues on a regular basis. Questions are expected, even encouraged. Concern is embraced as a vehicle for improvement. Solutions are developed from an in-depth knowledge of circumstances and an awareness of alternatives. Such knowledge is regularly sought, alternatives are routinely examined, actions are collaboratively determined, and their impacts are carefully assessed. Such is the nature of school renewal.

Renewal is not a one-shot deal. It is not something undertaken on Thursday and checked off a list the following Monday. It is not something that is ever "done." Instead, renewal is based on an eco-logical theory of change, one that takes into account the human and social nature of schooling and not just the rudimentary me-chanics. "One of the many advantages of an ecological theory," John Goodlad explains,

> is that it draws attention to what exists or is happening for purposes of information. What to do is not determined in advance but emerges out of diagnosis and consideration of alternatives. It may not be necessary to rip up the water system and replace it with another. Perhaps just a few leaks need to be repaired. Or, to use an analogy from schooling, it may not be necessary to install an entire new reading program; perhaps the teachers simply need more help with the present one. . . . Continuing inquiry into itself, then, is a condition necessary to the health of an educational ecosystem. Inquiry is enlightened by theory and so the explanatory power of the theory is critical to the adequacy of the data generated by inquiry.[3]

School renewal brings with it another benefit as well. It places responsibility for change in the hands of those who not only can and must make the changes, but who are likely to be most imme-diately affected by them. This means that support systems for every-one involved in the renewal process must be in place, and that in turn means that much of a school's existing regularities—those "fixed or recurring routines by means of which schools conduct their daily business, day after day, week after week"—must be changed if renewal is to become a part of school life.[4]

School Cultures

Culture is tenacious. If renewal is ever to become part of a school's culture, we must first recognize the power of that school's preexisting culture to preserve and perpetuate itself. Generally speaking, anthropologists tend to agree on three general characteristics of culture, each contributing to its self-preservation. First, culture is not something that individuals are born with, like the innate understanding of the sucking or nursing motion. Rather, culture is acquired. Teachers new to a school know this well. They quickly discover, for example, how powerful a cultural socialization process can be as others instruct them: *This is how we act in faculty meetings. This is how we spend our nonteaching time. This is how we interact with classroom aides or preservice teachers. This is how we support or disagree with one another. This is how we conduct our business.*

Second, anthropologists tend to see culture as having many different facets, and each of these facets intersects with many others, weaving a sort of societal fabric. A school's policy on promotion and nonpromotion, for example, which can sometimes be based on deeply held beliefs and value systems, is likely to influence disciplinary policies as well as interactions with parents and hierarchies within the social structures of both students and teachers. This suggests that if only one aspect of culture is altered, practices and behaviors are likely to revert soon to their earlier state. Therefore, if we want to make educational renewal part of a school's culture, the entire culture must change in accordance with new goals and expectations. A piecemeal approach will most certainly fail.

Third, for most anthropologists, culture is widely shared among members of a community and thus works to set limits or boundaries on what is and isn't acceptable behavior. Hence, a teacher new to a school who chooses not to conform to certain preestablished patterns of behavior is fast made aware that she has violated the school's cultural order. Edward Hall notes the pervasiveness of this kind of culture when he writes,

> There is not one aspect of human life that is not touched and altered by culture. This means personality, how people express themselves (including shows of emotion), the way they think, how they move, how problems are solved. . . . However, like the purloined letter, it is frequently the most obvious and taken-for-granted and therefore the least studied aspects of culture that influence behavior in the deepest and most subtle ways.[5]

Educational renewal is not likely to succeed in a school culture that remains resistant to change or that is unprepared to take the risks that change of such magnitude demands.

A school's culture can be said to reside most deeply in the less visible value and belief systems that influence behaviors. It is at this level that change is most difficult, and most necessary. In fact, one of the reasons that educational renewal has proven so effective is that, when it is successful, it works at the level of a school's culture. Referring to A Study of Schooling, Paul Heckman describes what are termed *regularities*—cultural norms that work, in this case, against school renewal: "Teachers in most schools remain isolated from one another. They do *not* discuss significant classroom problems and seek collegial solutions to them. . . . They spend little time talking substantively to one another about what they do in their classrooms." It is worth noting that a school's physical structures— which usually reflect particular cultural values and beliefs—often exacerbate such problems in that they tend to encourage isolation and stifle creative thinking about curriculum and pedagogy. In contrast to this, Heckman describes some of the cultural characteristics that researchers identified as indicative of successful renewal efforts:

> Principal leadership focused on the ways the principal handled conflict resolution, inspired the staff to work hard, promoted risk-taking, and showed personal competence. Staff cohesiveness reflected the degree to which the teachers viewed each other positively regarding the ways that they worked together. They perceived

a joining of the minds. They looked to each other for help and they received that help. . . . They did not drift from one problem to another without solving the initial problem.[6]

A renewing culture requires open channels of communication among its various members and components. Careful attention must be paid to the myriad connections among systems, structures, values, beliefs, and behaviors that combine to create and sustain a school's culture. It is for this reason that renewal is such a challenging strategy to employ. It is also for this reason that renewal can succeed where other approaches have failed.

Constructing a Body of Knowledge

Chapter One presented a condensed history of a series of initiatives launched in the second half of the twentieth century that were designed to provide understanding of both how educational change does or does not take place and how the business of schooling and the education of educators is conducted. Only one of the writers of this book took part in all of the initiatives described. Indeed, each initiative was carried out largely by a new group of colleagues.[7]

The fact that several colleagues moved on from one initiative into the next is in itself a tribute to the power of renewal. The body of learning about change, schooling, and the education of educators was preserved and then grew over time. It infused each subsequent undertaking, where it was used and evaluated, cast aside, reformulated, or strengthened. The newcomers to initiatives became, in a way, members of a "we" of both the present and the past; in so doing they advanced a continuing legacy of renewal. As we— the present writers—wrote in the Preface, our use of "we" embraces a much larger collectivity of participants whose work we hope to be representing faithfully. In most of what follows in this chapter we revisit the chronology of Chapter One as though all three of us were part of it, this time emphasizing what this larger "we" learned about processes of renewal. Although the institutions involved are educational ones and all of the players are educators, we believe that the individual and cultural renewing we describe is relative to a wide range of human settings and their stewards.

The idea of developing a renewing culture within educational settings was not born fully formed. Nor were all the complexities and implications of developing such a culture fully understood at the outset. What became clear early on in the work that led up to the creation of the Agenda for Education in a Democracy was that no genuine change strategy would ever be effective if it were not built on a solid, tried-and-true foundation. In practical terms, this meant constructing a body of knowledge that would provide a sort of road map to guide what we began to refer to as a strategy for change that is a fundamental component of the Agenda.

One early contributor to that body of knowledge was experienced with the Atlanta Area Teacher Education Service (AATES), a collaborative effort of six rapidly growing school districts and six colleges and universities in Georgia. The AATES was created to upgrade the qualifications of practicing teachers after World War II. This early renewal effort, which took place before the work described in Chapter One, provided John Goodlad and his colleagues with important insights into the conditions necessary to foster ongoing, self-generating school improvement. Three particular aspects of the AATES collaboration have since become virtually commonplace in educational change strategies.

The first lesson AATES provided was that *collegial efforts really do matter*. The good work of individuals may lead to personal growth, but they are unlikely to effect changes beyond themselves. Only an extraordinary egotist would consider changing a school alone. Therefore, if renewal is to take root in a school, a core group of teachers and the principal have to be engaged in the ongoing activity. Such teamwork is especially critical in the early stages of the renewal process.

The second lesson the AATES provided was that certain kinds of planning and preparation are necessary to launch any change effort. For example, intensive study is not to be undertaken at five o'clock in the afternoon when everyone is exhausted. Instead, it was realized, the core group has to be deliberately and formally provided with time away from classrooms and students to engage in the kind of sustained dialogue and reflection needed to begin to develop a culture of renewal.

This second lesson generated another. For school renewal to begin to take root, communication between core groups and others engaged in similar work have to be made commonplace. People who are involved in comparable work but are emotionally distanced from specific issues can provide new ideas and ask the kinds of provocative questions that can help move things forward. This kind of networking is commonly so much a part of our personal lives that we often don't recognize its power. It is viewed by many groups of workers as necessary to their being up-to-date in their fields. Cancer researchers, for example, routinely correspond with and publish their findings for the benefit of one another. Doctors and lawyers regularly discuss difficult cases with their peers. Wooden boat builders come thousands of miles to share the state of their craft with others. It makes sense that educators would do the same.

These findings were "road tested" many years ago. From the early 1950s into the 1960s, for instance, John Goodlad directed the Englewood Project in Florida. It was a unique and innovative undertaking. Teachers at the Englewood Elementary School progressed steadily into organizing and teaching multigrade, then multiage, and eventually nongraded classrooms. In doing this, considerable care was taken to heed the lessons learned from seeking to effect schoolwide change through the AATES. The Englewood Project not only confirmed the merit and importance of these findings, it also added two new criteria to what was becoming a growing body of knowledge.

First, a culture that supports risk taking and open discussion of experimentation is far more likely to engender improvement than one that overtly or covertly rewards control and predictability. In other words, a school's culture can do more than simply resist change; it can also be a potent force *for* change, given the proper conditions. This lesson has some subtle implications. Most important, it cautions against viewing a school's preexisting culture as a hurdle to be overcome or an obstacle to be circumvented—a view commonly held by proponents of school reform. Instead, it underscores the importance of directly engaging the school's culture as an ally in the overall change strategy. Given the tenaciousness of culture, such an approach is challenging but essential.

The Englewood Project also demonstrated the importance of a supportive infrastructure. Such an infrastructure should do two basic things. First and quite obviously, it should encourage everyone involved to work together in defining and creating the best possible conditions to put in place. Second, to be supportive this infrastructure must provide the resources and support mechanisms necessary to the renewing process. All the data, discussing, reflecting, planning, revising, shaping, and cajoling in the world are not going to improve our schools if we don't provide the resources and other necessary support apparatuses to shape ideas into realities. This too may seem quite obvious, but it is a lesson that bears repeating, because—whether in the schools, the federal government, or the United Nations—time and again we find the best of intentions thwarted by failure to provide the support necessary to see them through.

These lessons were later put to work in Southern California in 1966, when John Goodlad and a new set of colleagues put together the League of Cooperating Schools (LCS), a network of eighteen schools in eighteen districts joined in a long-term commitment to cultivating individual and institutional renewal. Guided by development of an inquiry process referred to as DDAE (dialogue, decision, actions, and evaluation), each school radically changed the way the faculty conducted school business.[8] (In retrospect, the DDAE process proved to be perhaps the single-most important vehicle for school renewal.) The way this process worked was that, in addition to meetings among principals and their faculties, the principals themselves met monthly as a group to discuss their work, while staff members of an independent "hub" (loosely connected with a major university and supported by a philanthropic foundation) worked with teachers and administrators to address their own specific problems. Mechanisms of technical support were put in place, including direct linkages with hub staff members; newsletters providing, among other information, research summaries in areas of shared interest; League conferences; opportunities for small groups with specific problems to meet; periodic meetings of superintendents; and formal systems to collect and disseminate data.

All LCS schools formally agreed that their efforts would be subjected to study. This resulted in the Study of Educational Change and School Improvement (SECSI). Among its many findings, the SECSI revealed that those processes that were most critical to changing the regularities of schooling—inquiry, for example—were the least understood. As a result, they were among the most difficult processes to implement. Not surprisingly, processes that were viewed, on the one hand, as critical but, on the other hand, as almost impossible to implement tended to be those that were most neglected. Consequently, some familiar regularities were too often left untouched.

It became apparent that bridges joining schools and the university were essential to critical inquiry. Unfortunately, it also became apparent that colleges and universities were less likely to view such relationships as vital to their interests, and therefore less likely to work hard at maintaining them. This probability suggested that special care had to be taken at the outset to overcome preexisting attitudes and to ensure that everyone involved fully understood the reasons for and benefits to be derived from such collaborations.

Two subsequent studies were soon to make their own important contributions to the body of knowledge that was emerging and that would eventually lead to the development of the Agenda for Education in a Democracy. The first was A Study of Schooling, with findings, conclusions, and recommendations reported in *A Place Called School*. The second was the Study of the Education of Educators (SEE). The SEE findings were reported in *Teachers for Our*

Nation's Schools.[9] These two studies of carefully selected settings nationwide contributed significantly to the substance of the Agenda, which in turn has been implemented over subsequent years in the National Network for Educational Renewal (NNER).

A Study of Schooling involved massive descriptions of thirty-eight elementary, middle, and secondary schools and more than a thousand classrooms. It presented a picture of schools in which well-intended individuals worked in isolation from one another, usually without the support necessary to improve either school or classroom practices. In addition, researchers routinely found many disengaged students, frustrated or complacent teachers, and administrators without the knowledge, skills, or background to effect more than rudimentary change. The study confirmed the critical role that a college or university could play in school renewal, especially with respect to providing alternatives to existing practices and the analytical skills necessary for research relevant to improvement.

Researchers came to realize that the juxtaposition of the action-oriented culture of the school and the inquiry-oriented culture of the university promised to shake loose the calcified practices of each institution (for example, how teachers teach and how they are prepared to teach). In the schools, it was noted, educators were accustomed to being told they needed to change. In fact, this expectation was seen as embedded in the school culture. Teacher educators, on the other hand, were assumed to be the rightful originators and proponents of school change (while, of course, remaining largely unchanged in their own practices). Nevertheless, those who conducted the study remained convinced that, once achieved, school-university partnerships would offer the real promise of stimulating collaborative inquiry into both the problems of the schools and the relevance of various collegiate and university research paradigms. Hope for the success of such collaboration was found in the observation that the agenda of instructional, curricular, and organizational improvements needed in the schools and the relevance of teacher education and research programs to schools of education overlapped. It was an insight that suggested that, with careful guidance, mutual self-interests might be employed to over-come resistance to change.

One question continually troubled the researchers. "Which comes first," they wondered, "good schools or good teacher-education pro-grams?" There were good arguments on each side of the debate, but none carried the day. Eventually they came to realize that the answer was that good schools and good teacher education programs had to develop simultaneously—in concert with each other. "We can't have good schools without good teachers," they realized. "And we can't have good teachers without good schools in which to prepare them." It didn't matter whether the horse or the cart came first; both were needed. To repeat what Goodlad has pointed out, "There must be a continuous process of educational renewal in which colleges and uni-versities, the traditional producers of teachers, join schools, the recip-ients of the products, as equal partners in the simultaneous renewal of schooling and the education of educators. The sooner the process begins, the sooner we will have good schools."[10]

Achieving Symbiotic Simultaneous Renewal

Simultaneous renewal, as used here, means parallel improvement efforts: two separate entities renewing themselves at more or less the same time. But simultaneous renewal does not necessarily have to mean *symbiotic* renewal. Positive symbiotic renewal is what oc-curs when two entities—a school and a college of education, for example—generate improvements as a result of their interactions with one another. Needless to say, symbiotic renewal presents a much more formidable challenge than does simultaneous renewal.

The first iteration of the NNER (1986–1990) focused primar-ily on schools and their renewal in an intended partnership with universities. University faculties comfortably took on the role of providing service to schools thought to need their help. It was a familiar role for university faculty members to assume. For one thing, it placed them, as experts, in a somewhat superior position, charitably lending a helping hand to their troubled colleagues.

However, anointing "experts" was never the intent of the founders of the NNER. John Goodlad, in part as a result of his work with the League of Cooperating Schools, was well aware of the seductive nature of helping others, rather than joining with them, in the process of creating a renewing culture: "So long as we remained in the somewhat missionary, giving role, there was little or no need to confront ourselves. The expert role is an attractive, tempting one," he explained.[11] Thus, by initially emphasizing *school* renewal, the NNER had unintentionally encouraged a "helping role" on the part of university faculties. It was another lesson learned.

The formulation of the necessary conditions for excellence in teacher education (presented in the propositions we called *postulates*, referred to in Chapter Two), resulting in large part from SEE findings, would eventually eliminate any complacency on the part of university participants. To work properly, renewal had to involve *both* schools and universities, on equal footing. No one could be exempted or allowed to stand apart from or above the renewal process. This requirement presented another problem in that, in this first iteration of the NNER, a number of the colleges and universities involved had signed on thinking that their role would be primarily an advisory one. To address this issue, NNER settings were asked to reexamine their commitment to *simultaneous* renewal and, if they were interested in continuing their involvement, to reapply to the NNER. As a result, the second iteration of the NNER conveyed the message that renewal had to involve everyone and could not be centered on just the schools.

In retrospect, this reconfiguration of the NNER may have shifted the onus of change somewhat from the schools to the colleges and universities, with K–12 teachers and administrators only too happy to see college and university faculties needing *their* expertise. In a critique of school-university relationships, professor of curriculum and instruction Martin Haberman writes,

> Public school people regard college people as too theoretical and more concerned with analysis than solutions, not capable of working within legal structures, incapable of hard work during regularly

scheduled business hours. College people perceive public school people as too conservative in accepting research or responding to great social problems; fearful of superiors; of lower intelligence, status, and education. . . . In truth, both groups are experts in maintaining their own organizations and espousing radical reforms in the other.[12]

Years earlier, Goodlad and his colleagues had come to realize that authentic engagement in school renewal processes requires new skills and knowledge from university participants as well as from those working in the schools. For renewal to become a successful process, both parties have to be willing to grow into new roles. "The important point is that we did not become expert in the teachers' and principals' roles or they in ours. It became more and more recognized, I think, perhaps intuitively, that a symbiosis likely to produce synergy depends not only on mutuality but also on difference, not similarity, in roles, skills, abilities, and satisfactions. *Unless true distinctiveness exists and is recognized, by definition there can be no symbiosis.*"[13] This realization raised two questions. First, if symbiotic, simultaneous renewal was possible, where was it most likely to occur? This led to a second question: What structures would support and encourage symbiotic, simultaneous renewal?

With these questions in mind, it was suggested that NNER settings should create a conceptual, not necessarily a physical, place to bring together everyone involved in preparing future educators. In addition to teachers and administrators from partnering schools, this meant involving university faculty members from departments of arts and sciences as well as from departments of education. Benefiting from the resulting broad range of ideas and expertise, this group would then be able to collaborate more effectively on improving the preparation of educators.[14]

It was an idea that made particularly good sense in light of the SEE findings. The SEE data left little doubt about the near-absence of conditions necessary to foster healthy teacher education programs. Findings included inadequate funding, lack of an articulated mission regarding the role of good schools in a just society, rare or no connections between schools of education and arts and science departments (where most of a teacher's coursework occurs), and equally poor relationships with schools (where preservice teachers complete required field experience).

The SEE data brought to light another concern as well. For renewal to work effectively in the programs that prepare tomorrow's teachers, educators in the arts and sciences would need to be just as involved in the process as those in departments of education. But there were no existing structures that could accommodate such a change strategy. To make such collaboration possible, the idea of creating a *center of pedagogy* was born.

Simply put, a center of pedagogy is a place where the three primary groups of teacher educators (arts and sciences faculty, P–12 educators, and teacher education faculty) collaborate in the work of building curriculum, field experiences, and the structures that produce good teachers. Ideally, no one group should be allowed to dominate a center of pedagogy. Leadership responsibilities must be assumed by all.

To be sure, centers of pedagogy have been slow to develop within the NNER. Given the difficulties inherent in implementing such an unconventional strategy, this is hardly surprising. Descriptions of centers of pedagogy in progress show that the concept can differ significantly from one setting to another.[15] Faculty and administrators from education, the arts and sciences, and partnering schools, for example, govern the center at New Jersey's Montclair State University. Public school teachers who work with preservice teachers are members, as are the university's arts and sciences professors who work with preservice teachers. Many of the latter have joint appointments with their home department and the center. Montclair's Center of Pedagogy has an independent operating budget and is specifically and formally charged with overseeing the preparation of educators. Utah's Brigham Young University, however, houses the Center for the Improvement of Teacher Education and Schooling (CITES). Unlike Montclair, CITES does not have governing authority over teacher education programs; instead, it invites, persuades, and creates opportunities for collaboration among interested parties. It does have a governing board comprising the partnering superintendents, the state's superintendent of schools, the university's academic vice president for undergraduate education, an executive director, and the college of education's dean. An executive management team includes arts and sciences representation and directs much of the center's work. CITES regularly holds seminars and creates opportunities for members to come together to learn from one another and discuss common concerns.

Much of the preparation of future educators takes place on college or university campuses. However, the part of that preparation that is consistently most highly valued by new teachers is what takes place during the hands-on field experience and internships in nearby schools. It is in these schools that future educators learn to determine the limits of what is possible, and where they decide how much of their "book learning" actually applies to the work of teaching.

It bears repeating that what is done in one location can easily be undone in another. Thus, when a college or university curriculum fails to consider adequately the day-to-day realities confronting teachers in the public schools (as it has sometimes been done in the past), new teachers will naturally favor the experiential wisdom and practice of classroom teachers over the experiences of others—for better or worse. Conversely, when teachers in the schools cease to benefit from new research in their field, opportunities to improve schooling and the preparation of educators are lost. As a result, in addition to centers of pedagogy, a second necessary structure for effective renewal of both schooling and educator preparation programs is the *partner school* or *professional development school* (PDS). This is where university teacher educators work with practicing teachers to develop the field experiences of preservice teachers. It is, in other words, where the curriculum of professional preparation becomes grounded in contemporary school realities.

In hindsight, the partner school is perhaps an idea whose time has come. In fact, several different groups in the mid- to late-1980s recommended the development of partner schools. The Holmes Group, a collection of one hundred deans from the nation's research institutions, did so in response to intense public criticism of schools and new teachers' preparation for them. The Carnegie Forum, a program of the Carnegie Corporation of New York, was created to examine links between the nation's economic strength and its schools. During that same period, work was under way at the Center for Educational Renewal to develop a deeper understanding of ecological change in the context of schooling and teacher education renewal. Each of these groups promoted somewhat different versions of schools wherein cohorts of preservice teachers would study with master teachers and wherein university faculty members would become part of the school's faculty, learning from and with them.[16]

The theory behind and expectations for partner schools are chronicled in Richard Clark's *Effective Professional Development Schools* and in John Goodlad's *Educational Renewal*.[17] In both books the partner school is viewed as a primary vehicle for the renewal of both schools and educator preparation programs. After all, it is in partner schools that college and university education faculty members can study the realities of schooling and see how new ideas can affect practice. It is in partner schools that teachers can learn to inquire into their own work and to improve the development of those who are preparing to teach. And it is in partner schools that preservice teachers can learn to question the gaps between theory and practice, and to create opportunities for effective professional dialogue.

As the Agenda for Education in a Democracy grew increasingly focused, it became apparent that additional criteria for partner schools were needed. As a result, NNER settings were asked—and agreed—to commit themselves to five ideas:[18]

1. Partner schools need to ensure that all learners have equal access to knowledge; entrenched practices such as tracking are to be examined and, it is hoped, replaced by practices that benefit all students.

2. Partner schools need to commit to developing practices that recognize and honor the diversity within school populations, that prepare students for active engagement in a democratic society, and that promote social justice.

3. Partner schools need to ensure that, in addition to realizing their own personal growth, students have to learn to contribute to the nation's democratic systems as well as to its economic health.

4. Partner schools need to design decision-making processes that actually involve students, parents, and other stakeholders.

5. Partner schools have to look beyond the schoolhouse gate and work to create larger educative communities with an eye toward helping to develop a more just and sustainable society.

Creating successful partner schools would prove, of course, to be a formidable challenge. In her study of partner schools, Corinne Mantle-Bromley found that some of the most deeply embedded regularities of both schooling and teacher preparation—those that stand most directly in the way of renewal—often remain firmly entrenched in their respective institutions.[19] She found it rare, for example, that teachers had either the time or the opportunity to talk with their colleagues about their work. Appreciation of inquiry was sometimes expressed, but inquiry had not become routine in teachers' work, nor had it become a central contribution of most university faculty members working in the partner schools.

At the university, reward structures continue to value theory-laden journal publications over practice-centered learning and publication. With reward structures remaining unchanged, university faculty members who work in partner schools are gradually being replaced by adjunct faculty who come from strong *schooling* backgrounds and who bring a *schooling* (rather than an inquiry and theory) perspective to the work. But both groups need to be deeply involved.

More recently, as partner school relationships have begun to mature, new requisite conditions have emerged and received greater emphasis. However, reward structures, for instance, continue to reinforce existing organizational cultures. For teachers, rewards come primarily from their students, reinforcing the desire to focus their efforts primarily within the classroom. University faculty members, on the other hand, are rewarded for peer-reviewed journal publication, reinforcing the tendency to center their work within the university rather than in the schools. If school and university educators are to benefit from each other's knowledge and expertise, if they are really to learn from one another, then reward structures in both settings need to be changed.

Mantle-Bromley also points out that teachers, administrators, and staffs are not born with the skills needed to analyze and talk about their own work or the work of their colleagues, and that it is rare that discussions lead to reflection in or on practice and, when appropriate, actual changes in practice. The capacity for peers to value, provide, and receive feedback has not been cultivated in most educational settings. Ironically, this means that something that educators routinely do with (and often to) their students becomes new and sometimes even frightening when attempted with their colleagues.

Mantle-Bromley's study also revealed that collective inquiry continues to be problematic. In part this is because structures have not been created to provide the time it takes to inquire meaningfully into practice. It is also because teachers have not been convinced of the value of collective inquiry in improving practice. If inquiry is to become an integral part of the work teachers do, then the requisite skills and knowledge it requires have to be intentionally developed, and researchers need to demonstrate—in very practical ways—how inquiry can and does improve student learning.

Finally, Mantle-Bromley found that although those who have already helped create successful partnerships may readily acknowledge the benefits of engaging in the hard work of simultaneous renewal, such benefits are not always evident to newcomers. Therefore, those who are new to the partnership community must be carefully and deliberately mentored into the emerging culture of renewal if they are to contribute to its potential.

Strengthening the Culture of Renewal

In their examination of school-university collaboration as part of an initiative in strengthening and sustaining teachers in their careers, Paul Heckman and Corinne Mantle-Bromley concluded that partnership work has improved the preparation of preservice teachers—that is, graduates of partnership programs are better prepared for today's classrooms.[20] Some of the major reasons for this are that preservice teachers now spend more time actually working in classrooms with students, their university professors (at least those who work in the partner schools) are more attuned to the realities of today's classrooms and students, and the teachers with whom they work are more knowledgeable about the content of the university classes.

However, the study of school-university partnerships has to date revealed little that indicates that the partnerships have significantly loosened the calcified cultural regularities of either schools or universities. To wit, teachers remain isolated from one another, ongoing inquiry into practice is conducted only in fits and starts (awaiting changes in supporting value systems such as reward structures and schedules), teachers and teacher educators find it difficult to engage in conversations about practice when the practice is their own or is problematic. In short, the changes that have occurred may not yet be deep enough to alter the long-entrenched ways we conduct schooling. Nonetheless, there is now plenty of evidence to show that this partnering is producing significant improvement in the ways the two sets of institutions and the individuals involved in them conduct business.

School-university partnerships in general and partner schools specifically are the essential vehicles through which we may bring about simultaneous renewal. But they are not, in and of themselves, the goal. They are designed to chip away at the unproductive cultural artifacts of schooling and teacher preparation programs, and to try to replace them with more useful beliefs and behaviors. No individual or group of individuals working on the fringe of their institution can bring about cultural changes of magnitude on their own. The power of an organization's existing culture is far more likely to effect change in the individual than the individual is likely to affect change in the organization. Ultimately, the success of renewal efforts depends first and foremost on groups of individuals who can and are willing to commit the time and energy needed for the collaboration necessary to change.

Heckman and Mantle-Bromley propose three principles to help guide the future work of partnerships:

1. Participants must agree that the purpose of their partnership work is in part to challenge long-held beliefs and assumptions about teaching and learning.
2. Participants need to agree that it is everyone's responsibility to raise even the most basic questions about theory and practice.
3. Participants have to agree to work together and be willing to try new ideas.[21]

While such principles are easily stated and may even seem self-evident, they have nevertheless proven extremely difficult to implement.

Creating and sustaining a culture of renewal is difficult and demanding work. Success does not come about because of goodwill alone, although goodwill can certainly help. In the final analysis, success comes about because of a shared vision of what might be, combined with patience, resources, and political support. But unless participants are willing, as an integral part of their work, to question regularly their own and each other's practices, the best intentions and efforts are likely to result in only superficial changes, with the result that tomorrow's schools will end up looking much like the schools of today.

This culture of renewal, if it is to thrive, must be cared for in the larger context. A renewing school within a district that is hardened against change will eventually revert to the state it was in before. New teachers who have learned the power of collaboration and inquiry will continue those practices only if they are teaching in situations where others are either already committed to such practices or are willing to approve and adopt them.

Good gardening practices have much in common with educational renewal and can be used to illustrate several key renewal concepts: the power of observation, the need to inquire routinely, and the importance of context. But the metaphor eventually breaks down. Happily, that breaking down is equally illustrative in that it indicates what we must change if we are to create and nurture good schools and good teachers.

Gardeners regularly toss plants into the compost pile: this one is too leggy, that one requires too much water or is too susceptible to disease. Gardeners don't expect every plant to survive. Some even anticipate winterkill and loss over time. They give up on some plants; they decide which are good and which are bad (and label the bad ones "weeds"). They ignore the plants they don't like. Gardeners can be very set in their ways. Some only like roses, others use dangerous pesticides and fertilizers that keep their lawns weed free and florescent green but which destroy our oceans and rivers. Others fail to consider their neighbor when they carelessly plant a tree that will eventually shade the neighbor's vegetable garden.

Consider for a moment how many of our current educational practices parallel this nonrenewing side of gardening. The fact is that too many children are seen as expendable and are set aside where they can be comfortably ignored. Too many are told that they are simply too much trouble to deal with, that their emotional requirements are too demanding, or that their "condition" upon arrival is poor and that they will never prosper. Too many new teachers begin their careers agreeing that what currently exists is, as singer-songwriter Steve Earle puts it, "the best we can do."[22]

The garden that simultaneous renewal creates should not be one of carefully controlled beauty, where shades of crimson stems purposefully complement the neighboring leaves of ocher. Rather, the garden of renewal should be a human enterprise, a place of wonder and discovery, where every day brings about new understandings and new insights, and holds new promise.

Educational renewal asks that we dare to envision what doesn't currently exist: systems that view every student as precious and worthy of the best schooling possible, systems that support teachers in their quest for what works for each child, and systems that hold the preparation of future educators as a highly valued, moral endeavor. To bring about these kinds of systemic change, wherein university and school educators work together toward collaboratively determined goals, the "we" of simultaneous educational renewal (teachers and other school-based educators; administrators; teacher educators and counselor, special education, and administrator educators; arts and sciences professors; and so on) must make changes in our daily work and in the systems that support and connect to our work. The road ahead may be steep but it is also wide. There is plenty of room for all of us.

Chapter Seven

Leadership for Educational Renewal

"We are not a society that devotes much of our substantial resources to our students or children," write Daniel Liston and Kenneth Zeichner in *Culture and Teaching*. "Our society is class-based, racially divided, and essentially masculinist in its orientation. Greed and consumerism are at its core. The accumulation of wealth and status are its motivating forces."[1] Although we agree with this dispiriting and bleak assessment, it is one that can leave those who envision a healthier, more just, and more equitable future feeling helpless, overwhelmed, without hope.

Hope, we believe, is essential to human survival. Without hope we would have little use for tomorrow. We would have no *need* of tomorrow. The Agenda for Education in a Democracy is about fostering, nurturing, and championing hopes for a brighter tomorrow, whatever the circumstances in which we may presently find ourselves, whatever the odds against realizing our collective dreams and ambitions.

In fact, the Agenda is built on hopes. It is built on the hope that the number of educational leaders who understand how fundamentally our schools must change continues to increase. It is built on the hope that politicians will soon see that carrot-and-stick reforms do little to alter the deep structures of schooling or the conditions that economically poor children face every day. It is built on the hope that society will come to see that good test scores do not necessarily result in good neighbors or make good citizens.

In light of the problems deeply embedded in our society, as educators we feel we have a moral responsibility to act on our knowledge of child and adolescent development, of learning and teaching, of collaboration, and of renewal. To do anything less would be unconscionable, for such a failure would only support and prolong the very structures and norms that demean and devalue our nation's young.

It is as unrealistic to suggest that we can change our society by changing our schools as it is to suggest—as some have—that we can change our economy by changing our schools. Our schools cannot make or break our economy, nor can they "fix" racism or economic injustice.

But knowledge and awareness can be powerful. We did not really begin to deal with civil rights issues until the civil rights movement brought the crisis to national attention and citizens across the nation were forced to confront the ugly realities of racism. If we want to have a society that is aware of and responsive to the myriad problems we face, then we must intentionally create such a society. And that is where public education comes into the picture.

Youths who graduate from high schools ready to become meaningfully engaged citizens in a democratic society (with skills, for example, in literacy, knowledge acquisition, and persuasion, and with dispositions toward justice, compassion, and the common good) will be far better equipped to make positive changes in their own lives and those of their families and neighbors. The bottom line is simply that it is highly unlikely that our society will change for the better unless *all* of our nation's young are adequately prepared to assume the responsibilities of democratic citizenship— the tools for change. We cannot expect a better future for all by relegating authority to a privileged few whose primary qualifications are often the happenstance of birth.

For too long now our schools have failed to prepare most students for productive social and political engagement. In fact, this essential *public* purpose of schooling is rarely even on the radar screen of most politicians who influence education policy and instigate reform efforts. Unless those who are currently underserved and disenfranchised are made ready to participate in the decision-making processes that affect their lives and that shape the world around them, we as a nation will continue to suffer the indignity, deprivation, and injustices of a social and political system that largely benefits the prosperous few at the expense of a growing underclass. Such a failure to teach all children well is morally unacceptable; it robs them of enriching futures and jeopardizes the very freedoms that we, as Americans, so passionately claim as our democratic birthright.

Clearly things need to change. In many cases the needed changes are quite basic and straightforward. Students need to be involved with adults who care deeply for their well-being. They need to see adults struggling, just as they themselves do, to enact difficult changes. They need to see how inquiry processes can improve their lives. They need to feel the power and grace of equity and justice.

Those who go on to become teachers themselves need even more. They need to learn to continually hone their skills, methods, and techniques. They need to recognize and ultimately embrace the kind of humility that accompanies a willingness and prepared-ness to learn. Most important, future educators need to see the steps that follow both success and failure: more inquiry, more mea-sured experimentation, increased diversity of ideas, and new efforts toward improvement. These changes cannot be brought about without strong leadership. But the leadership that educational renewal requires is quite different from the hierarchical leadership usually associated with top-down, externally driven reform efforts.

The Need for Strong Leadership

In *Leading Minds*, Howard Gardner defines leaders as "persons who, by work and/or by personal example, markedly influence the behaviors, thoughts, and/or feelings of a significant number of their fellow human beings."[2] Gardner suggests that there are three levels of leadership influence. *Ordinary leaders* relate traditional stories in effective ways, but they do not seek change beyond the already existing commonplaces of the group. *Innovative leaders* bring new or different attention to stories that often have lain dormant. Although their stories are not new ones, they are stories that have been neglected or sometimes silenced.

Those unique individuals that Gardner calls *visionary leaders* are exceedingly rare. Visionary leaders create entirely new stories. What was before seen as impossible now becomes entirely and quite reasonably possible because of radically new ways of thinking or perceiving.

Our schools and our teacher education programs have not lacked leaders. Good people—those Gardner would call ordinary leaders—have long worked within existing systems and structures to provide the best schooling they can for children and youths. What we have lacked, however, are significant numbers of innovative leaders: those who are sufficiently dissatisfied with the current economic narrative of schooling (as we discussed in Chapter Four) that they embrace an alternative narrative of equity and freedom of the sort born alongside this country's democratic foundation. Such a narrative would be a hopeful narrative, one that dared to envision a better future for everyone. This narrative exists but has been conveniently swept into the dark corners of our nation's consciousness by those who do not share its values and who benefit handsomely by maintaining the injustices of the status quo.

As we are using it here, the word *narrative* (in this case, borrowed from the work of Neil Postman) corresponds, we think, to what Gardner refers to as *story*. Postman explains that "the purpose of a narrative is to give meaning to the world, not to describe it scientifically. The measure of a narrative's 'truth' or 'falsity' is in its consequences: Does the story provide people with a sense of personal identity, a sense of community life, a basis for moral conduct, explanations of that which cannot be known?"[3]

As Postman makes clear, narrative can powerfully influence our actions: "The question is not, Does or doesn't public schooling create a public? The question is, What kind of public does it create? A

conglomerate of self-indulgent consumers? Angry, soulless, direc-
tionless masses? Indifferent, confused citizens? Or a public imbued
with confidence, a sense of purpose, a respect for learning, and
tolerance?"[4]

Our schools today desperately need innovative leaders who can
dust off the narrative that implores creation of a thoughtful public,
as proposed by Thomas Jefferson, Horace Mann, John Dewey, and
many other distinguished scholars. We need innovative leaders
who are ready and willing to challenge the status quo, leaders who
can influence others in pursuit of schools that engage all students
in meaningful learning toward the ultimate purpose of creating a
thoughtful public willing and prepared to work toward a healthy
and just democracy.

Most of us feel the influence of leaders and their powerful
narratives daily. Religious leaders ask that we live our lives in accordance with their tenets. Marketing leaders, rarely seen but ubiqui-
tously felt, tell us that our personal identities are determined, at least
in part, by the car we drive, the clothes we wear, the brand of soda we
drink. Political leaders tell their stories as well. Taxes are imposed or
retracted, social programs are initiated or halted, and wars are started
because of their narratives.

Most of us are familiar with organizations that suffer from weak
leadership. Priorities shift with the wind, actions make no sense, a
fear of the unknown permeates the air. A strange paralysis seems to
descend upon leaderless or weakly led organizations. Many of us
have also experienced strong leadership that we believed to be
wrongheaded, even reprehensible. Adolf Hitler will always serve as
a reminder that leadership can all too easily promote immoral purposes. Leadership, like education, is itself value-neutral, but it can
be made to serve many different gods, many different narratives,
and many different ideas about tomorrow.

When leadership fails or is corrupted, the damage and decay it
causes affects all that it touches. Institutions and programs with
weak leadership either embrace every new fad that comes along or
they embrace nothing at all. Immoral and corrupt leaders have

condoned mediocrity, ignored flagrant misconduct, denied their charges valuable opportunities, hired unqualified and incompetent pals, hid or pocketed badly needed funds, favored timid and gullible employees over those who are creative and inspired, and worse. Poor leadership is always a problem for any institution or organization affected by it. For those engaged in educational renewal, it can be disastrous. This is why the Agenda for Education in a Democracy has long been committed to developing skilled leaders.

Our understanding of leadership for renewal in K–12 settings can be traced back to the Atlanta area effort to increase teachers' qualifications shortly after the end of World War II. From this undertaking we learned that a strong core group of teachers and an effective principal were sufficient to initiate a renewing culture. This work, called the Englewood Project (discussed in Chapter Six), showed that the principal needed to be responsible for communicating a strong and consistent vision (or narrative) to both the teachers and the community as a whole.

For new ways of operating to take hold, however, leadership needs to come predominantly from individual teachers. The Englewood Project suggested that while the principal can and indeed must articulate a vision for change, it is the teachers themselves who tend to be most effective at consolidating the kind of support needed to translate a vision into reality. The role of the principal then becomes to ensure that those who are taking on such leadership responsibilities receive the kind of support and encouragement they need to succeed.

The League of Cooperating Schools project (discussed in Chapters One and Six) demonstrated that if educational renewal was to remain a vital transformative force for schooling over the long haul, then top leadership—particularly school superintendents—would also need to understand and be supportive of the renewal efforts going on in their schools. In truth, the role of these leaders is partly to provide a protective buffer against forces that can work to counteract or overwhelm renewal strategies.

Leadership for renewal in higher education settings may be even more difficult than it is at the K–12 level. The culture of the university is one of independent thinking and scholarship, not of collaboration and unity. The university culture actively promotes faculty members as experts rather than as lifelong learners engaged in renewal processes. Entrenched reward structures within university systems serve only to support these values.

Whether leadership for renewal at the university level is the responsibility of the dean, the director of teacher education, or someone else, it is critical that this person have a well-defined vision of the renewal process and a good understanding of how vital the work of schools is to the effectiveness of educator preparation, as well as to the work of the university as a whole. This means that the narratives embraced by university leaders must consistently be powerful, coherent, and clearly articulated. Moreover, university leaders must be able to persuade faculty members across the disciplinary spectrum that the preparation of educators is a responsibility that needs to be shouldered by everyone, not just by those preparing teachers and other educators.

The work of simultaneous educational renewal also involves collaborations beyond school and university settings. As these two institutions come together in professional development schools (PDSs) or partner schools, educational leaders in both settings need to be able to work not just within their own organizations, but also in close collaboration with leaders of organizations that often are quite different from their own. Richard Clark has recently studied PDSs and his conclusions echo those of earlier studies. Clark has found that the design and implementation of PDSs require multiple leaders occupying different roles. One leader, for example, might be the person who initiates the relationship that becomes the PDS. That individual could be either at the university level or in the partner school. Another leader might be called a "boundary spanner." This would be a person who understands the cultures of both higher education and the schools and who has established credibility in both arenas.

Other leadership roles include the school principal who plays a key role in communicating a common vision and engaging more and more people in the renewal process. Teachers both in the schools and in the university who enlist the support and engagement of their peers are also essential leaders in educational renewal efforts. Parent and community group leaders can become informed and enthusiastic collaborators as well. As Clark writes, "Leaders are essential to creating an effective PDS." In fact, "Each of the steps . . . depends on effective leadership for realization."[5]

Another recent study of nine PDSs in four settings confirmed the importance of leaders at different levels and in different roles. Those PDSs whose principals placed the partnership at the center of their school's responsibilities engaged far more teachers in the work than did other principals. Teacher leaders and university faculty leaders were vital to programs where joint ownership and broad engagement were present, and university faculty members were more comfortable in their boundary-spanning roles when they felt strong support from their university leaders.[6]

In summarizing his review of studies and the efforts that have led to creation of the Agenda for Education in a Democracy, Kenneth Sirotnik states:

> One of the most consistent and enduring findings in the research on complex organizations is the importance of leadership at the top and the ability to clearly, authentically, and consistently communicate a mission, a vision, a sense of what the organization can and must be about. This appears to be essential to maintaining school-university partnerships. University presidents and deans, school superintendents and principals, partnership directors—these leaders need to be visible and clearly supportive of the partnership concept and effort.[7]

Clearly, innovative leadership—formal leadership at the top as well as less formal leadership within the institution—is vital to organizations intent on renewal.

What Makes a Good Leader?

It would be nice if there were a simple and concise list of the characteristics of successful leaders of educational renewal. Unfortunately, no such list exists. Nor could it, given the diversity of both effective leaders and the circumstances in which they work. It is easier to describe the job and its value than it is to describe the qualities of the person most ideally suited to do the job. Nevertheless, from the work of those who have studied leadership, some specific and fairly consistent qualities for effective leadership in educational renewal begin to emerge.

Gardner's study of leadership, for example, places central importance on the leader's story or narrative. Gardner found that "the ultimate impact of the leader depends most significantly on the particular story that he or she relates or embodies, and the receptions to that story on the part of audiences." He adds that "the stories of the leader—be they traditional or novel—must compete with many other extant stories; and if the new stories are to succeed, they must transplant, suppress, complement, or in some measure outweigh the earlier stories, as well as contemporary oppositional 'counterstories.'"[8]

Gardner also found that persuasive direct leaders (those in designated leadership positions such as principals or deans) live their lives in accordance with their stories. In other words, they need to lead by example. Such leaders model and embody the values and behaviors they are trying to instill in others, whether such values and behaviors are, for instance, open inquiry, risk taking, or simply valuing life as a learning process. Thus, leaders whose stories emphasize inquiry and reflection routinely engage in inquiry and reflection themselves if they want others to share their vision.

Wilma Smith, a former school superintendent, has practiced, studied, and written about the leader as a steward of the ecological whole of the school or educator preparation program. Smith sees formal or designated leaders as well as informal leaders as critical to the renewal process. She describes steward-leaders as people who create and support safe environments, who excel at developing civil discourse, who do not feel a need to control others, who constantly reflect on their own practice to ensure that it is in keeping with their mission, and who nurture a culture of inquiry and professional growth.[9]

Robert Patterson, Nicholas Michelli, and Arturo Pacheco, deans of schools or colleges of education in National Network for Educational Renewal (NNER) member institutions of higher education, studied and wrote about their own experiences in creating boundary-spanning centers of pedagogy within their institutions.[10] They found four common aspects to their efforts (each of which requires skilled leadership). First, each of the institutions had created a shared mission and responsibility for the preparation of educators. These leaders had persuasive stories and were both persistent and patient in bringing others into their stories. Second, the deans found a slow and deliberate building of trust among the various parties. They wrote about the critical roles played by their own faculties and the schools' faculties in bringing about this trust. Third, the authors found that governance structures were significantly influenced by the historical context of each institution. This meant that there was no one best way to create or govern a center of pedagogy. Leaders needed a good understanding of contextual nuances as they sought solutions appropriate to their own unique settings. Finally, to fund innovative centers of pedagogy, each of the institutions had to be able to use both internal and external sources that were sympathetic to the idea of establishing new structures to support such collaborations of schools, arts and sciences, and education faculties.

Effective leaders are those who deeply understand change processes and the supports essential to them. In his study of PDSs, Richard Clark found that not only do successful leaders bring strong intellectual grounding and communication skills to their work, but they also bring with them a deep understanding of resources and budgets that can be used to influence and support change strategies. It is notable that such leaders also anticipate and prepare for their own replacement, purposefully developing the necessary leadership skills in others with whom they work.[11]

In an examination of teacher leadership, three Connecticut researchers have described a number of characteristics of classroom teachers who have effectively contributed to school renewal efforts.[12] Perhaps the most important of these characteristics is the never-ending quest for innovation: specifically, new understanding, new insights, and better answers to (usually) old questions. Teachers who are effective leaders of renewal are those who consciously influence the thoughts and actions of their colleagues in ongoing improvement efforts and who engage in inquiry and reflection as a regular part of their work. This reflection tends to be proactive; that is, it is designed to produce a course of action. And these teachers assume that any resulting action will itself be examined and, quite likely, improved upon.

Although the unique qualities of those who lead effective renewal efforts are beginning to emerge, we still lack one critical component. If we want our schools' graduates to become thoughtful and engaged democratic citizens, we need to ask ourselves what skills and dispositions this democracy education should entail. Then, following Gardner's findings, we need to ask how educational renewal leaders would model and foster in others those particular skills and dispositions.

As discussed earlier, Roger Soder has given such matters considerable thought. We earlier presented his argument that a healthy democracy requires certain civic attributes that support it.[13] One of those attributes is trust. Imagine, for a moment, how much trust we extend to strangers every day and how frustrated and sometimes angry we become when that trust is violated. We trust, for example, that money we place in the bank will be available to us when we want it. We trust that our lights will come on when we flip the switch on the wall. We trust that our drinking water is relatively clean, and that our children are reasonably well cared for in school. Imagine what would happen if our trust in such things was found to be misplaced.

This kind of trust has correlates in our political and social structures and institutions. For example, we trust our leaders to be well informed, to act on our behalf, to recognize and serve the public good, and to uphold the tenets of democracy, among other things. Such trust is a necessary condition for a healthy democracy. It therefore makes sense that implementation of the Agenda for Education in a Democracy requires leaders who are capable not only of modeling such trust themselves but also of developing that kind of trust in others.

Successful leaders in educational renewal efforts tend to share other qualities as well. They tell persuasive stories. They make the values embedded in their stories their own. They see and care for the ecological whole. They nurture conditions that support that whole. They build trust among stakeholders and are sensitive to the unique context of their own institutions. They model and foster in others the skills and dispositions necessary to a healthy democracy. And rather than assume that they already have all the answers, they use their understanding of change processes in their work with others to examine data, determine next steps, and study the impact of those steps.

A Leadership Program for Renewal

Roger Soder reminds us of an age-old problem when he writes, "We know that organizational change takes a long time, and we know that we want *our* changes, carefully effected with much effort, to last a long time. At the same time, there is a lot of mobility, a lot of administrative turnover. Leaders leave; other leaders succeed them. The process of succession, part of a larger culture, has its own expectations, rituals, and rules—its own culture."[14]

We realized long ago that if those of us at the Center for Educational Renewal and, later, the Institute for Educational Inquiry were to support and influence renewal efforts in the various settings of the NNER, strong leadership development would be extremely important. Especially troublesome was the frequent turnover in top administrative positions, both in institutions of higher education and in the schools.[15] The SEE study showed, for example, an average tenure of 6.6 years for education deans, with the position often filled on an acting basis or left vacant. Provost or academic vice president positions experienced even greater turnover. And institution presidents—those with the lowest rate of turnover—were in their positions, on average, for only eight years. At any given time, the likelihood of any of these positions being filled by someone new, someone leaving, or someone "acting" was quite high. The possibility of there being well-established relationships among those in these positions, along with a shared commitment to a well-articulated vision of educator preparation, was slight. The situation in schools, as the Study of Schooling data made clear, wasn't much better.

The lesson is clear: leadership cannot reside solely in "positional" leadership if long-term changes are to take root. Not only do leaders need to be constantly developing other leaders who can, if need arises, replace them; they need also to seek and support leadership outside conventionally recognized positions. If efforts to change the deep structures of schooling and educator preparation programs are going to continue during periods of leadership transition, then alternative kinds of leadership need to exist outside of and in tandem with formal leadership structures.

Central to the development of diversified leadership has been the IEI's Leadership Associates Program in Seattle. NNER settings have nominated university professors and administrators, counselors, special educators, and public school teachers and administrators to participate in this yearlong program of discussion and analysis of educational renewal.

Others have described the Leadership Associates Program in detail.[16] Here, rather than repeat information regarding structure, curriculum, and impact, we instead present the conceptual basis for the Leadership Associates Program: what we were trying to accomplish, what constraints and opportunities resulted from critical decisions, and what we have learned from this effort to support the development of leadership for educational renewal in the various NNER settings and beyond.

The stated purpose of the Leadership Associates Program is "To empower a cadre of leaders deeply committed to the Agenda who will work to carry out the vision of renewing simultaneously America's schools and the education of educators."[17] This statement reflects the iterative process of designing, implementing, and redesigning the program itself. The phrase "cadre of leaders," for example, required that we think carefully about who ought to participate in the program. Would it be only for those in formal leadership positions? Or would it be for those coming into positional leadership roles as well? Or perhaps it should include those in informal leadership roles. If the latter were the case, then how would teachers respond to working alongside deans and school superintendents?

Knowing that renewal requires leadership in both formal and informal positions, we decided not to restrict participation to any one group. Given our belief in multiple perspectives and the importance of learning from and with those who sometimes view the world differently than we do, we sought a balance among arts and sciences, public school, and school or college of education faculty members and administrators. This decision required that we flatten traditional hierarchies within each group, that we strive to establish trust between and among these groups, and that we work to ensure the full participation of everyone involved.

If we were to develop leaders who were "deeply committed to the Agenda," as the statement of purpose asserts, then we would have to be prepared to teach the components of the Agenda for Education in a Democracy to each new Leadership Associates Program cohort. But could we present information and design exploratory activities that would inspire experts (in classroom teaching, for example, or in the administration of a school district or department of arts and sciences) to look at longstanding issues in new and compelling ways? Was it even realistic to think that out of such an experience a strong commitment to the Agenda would arise among members of such a diverse group?

Such considerations led us to select readings that we hoped would be new for at least the vast majority of participants. Recognizing the value of learning from one another's experiences, we strongly encouraged all participants to share their views and ideas in as honest, direct, and open a manner as possible.

We determined that the Leadership Associates Program had to be grounded in a specific context and in specific content. Thus, readings were selected and activities were designed on the basis of their relevance to the four moral dimensions of the Agenda's mission.

In addition, we deliberately employed pedagogical techniques that we hoped would be later replicated in the settings: discussion of issues based on data and on authors' claims and positions; examination of issues with a moral lens; heterogeneous grouping; and large and small group activity among them. Also, the decisions we made concerning the conduct and content of the Leadership Associates Program were never carved in stone. Readings and activities were constantly evaluated and updated. Participants regularly suggested new readings for future cohorts. Each year saw significant evolutionary changes in the program.

As expected, commitment to the Agenda for Education in a Democracy developed over time. Not surprisingly, such commitment varied considerably in degree from one person to another. Some participants have said that the program was the single most important professional development experience of their lives. Others have rated the program highly but have said that its impact on their work was only moderate. Most participants have said that the Leadership Associates Program succeeded in deepening their understanding of, appreciation for, and commitment to the ideas and values that form the Agenda.

The last half of the Leadership Associates Program's statement of purpose indicates that Agenda leaders are "to carry out the vision of renewing simultaneously America's schools and the education of educators." It is a statement that raises difficult questions and has complex implications: Is the simultaneous renewal agenda sufficiently powerful to persuade diverse educators of its fit with our

nation's schooling needs and with each of their spheres of influence? How will these educators go about implementing such a
broad agenda in settings that differ greatly? What support systems
need to be in place at each setting to ensure success? How might
the IEI itself best support the participants as they move back into
their setting roles? These questions—and many others—led to several design features that have remained integral to the Leadership
Associates Program throughout its tenure.

First, participants have been expected to engage in some form of
inquiry, using ideas from the Agenda for Education in a Democracy
to study some compelling aspect of schooling or educator preparation
in their own settings. These projects have varied considerably over
the years, but a focus on critical inquiry into the status quo has always
been a central component. Such study has led to changes that take
into account issues of equity and justice and historical context. Such
changes have in turn led to new inquiries, initiating or furthering the
process of renewal in the participants' settings.

These projects have had some very real impact on what goes on
in schools and teacher preparation programs. For example, in several cases inquiry projects have led to the creation of new courses.
Other projects have looked at where prospective teachers can substantively learn about poverty and its impact on children. Still
other research has led, in one case, to a superintendent's shaping of
his vision for—and narrative about—schooling, and in other cases,
to new selection processes for teacher preparation programs.

Another constant feature of the Leadership Associates Program
is the search for ways to create useful feedback mechanisms. In
some years, participants have had opportunities to visit other settings to learn about their particular problems and discuss commonalities and differences in their approaches to their work.
Participants have routinely been required to present their inquiry
projects to their cohort members (and often to a much larger audience). These presentations have resulted in discussions that have
often led participants to formulate future inquiry.

A third feature of the program has been efforts to keep program
graduates in contact with one another in order to strengthen the

network itself as well as their connections to the work of the IEI. Once participants complete the program, they are often called upon to help the IEI implement new initiatives, to participate in discussions, and sometimes to serve as facilitators of future iterations of the Leadership Associates Program.

As of the summer of 2002, ten cycles of the Leadership Associates Program had been completed. In most years, a single cohort of fifteen to eighteen individuals from various NNER settings has participated in three to four sessions (each session three to four days long) of intensive study of the Agenda. But during four of these years, the IEI decided instead to work with two cohorts simultaneously. At certain times the two cohorts would join to form a larger single group of about thirty individuals. During these years, the IEI experimented with bringing in teams of three participants from each setting as a way to try to increase the program's impact on a setting's institutions.

To date, more than two hundred people have participated in the IEI's Leadership Associates Program. Many of these individuals have gone on to help deliver similar programs to educational leaders in their own settings.[18] Thus the program has served as a primary vehicle for strengthening leadership for renewal in all of the NNER settings. The program has also been instrumental in helping settings to maintain their commitment to the renewal agenda during times of leadership turnover and transition. The program has, in short, helped create a nucleus of educational leaders who speak a common language, share a common set of experiences and a common purpose, and enjoy the support of a network of dedicated colleagues.

Education for Everyone: Preparing for the Future

Although we believe that the Leadership Associates Program has played a vital role in the progress that has been made within the NNER settings, in the spirit of the agenda of renewal we continue to search for ways to improve it. As a result, for the first time in ten years, after participants of the 2001–02 Leadership Associates

Program completed their study with IEI, we did not solicit nominations for participants for the following year. Instead, we committed ourselves to a year of study and evaluation during which we could reflect on our progress to date, consider possible contextual changes, and generally redesign the program. To help us do this, we brought together participants from earlier years to talk about their experiences and to share their thoughts for improving future iterations.

In addition, we have conducted an evaluation of the impact of our work on individual settings over the last three years. This evaluation included a survey and setting-based focus group interviews. Senior associates of the IEI regularly gathered to discuss our findings and to explore the implications of those findings for improving future Leadership Associates Programs.

It has become apparent that changing circumstances will continue to require that we make changes in the Leadership Associates Program. The most notable change has been in how the Agenda has been understood at the various NNER settings. Initially, the Leadership Associates Program was designed to serve as a basic introduction to the Agenda. But in more recent years the range of participants' experience in and knowledge of the Agenda has come to vary considerably. While some participants, usually those new to their settings, may still need an introduction to our common work, Leadership Associates Program participants now often include those who have been working in various ways with the Agenda for some time and are now ready for a quite different level of study. Simultaneously accommodating the needs of both groups will not be an easy undertaking.

A second change we have had to face is political. The federal government has, in the last several years, assumed greater control of both schools and the preparation of educators. High stakes testing and issues of accountability now dictate the work of many educators. It has become increasingly difficult for leaders to present visions of schooling that counter the current narrative of testing and accountability. We agree that schools and educator preparation must be held to high standards of learning. We agree that educators must be accountable for their students' learning. And returning to the beginning of this chapter, we know that schools cannot solve a society's ills. Labeling schools, teachers, and students as failures will not bring about the long-term changes that our schools so desperately need.

Good schools emerge from supportive environments, from learning communities, from the care and nurture of the whole. By making it possible for educators themselves to take responsibility for their students' learning, to create vehicles for ongoing inquiry, and to work with others in both similar and dissimilar roles, we believe we are supporting the kind of efforts that will lead to schools that can consistently serve all children well.

As we implement a new version of the Leadership Associates Program (or perhaps multiple versions addressing multiple needs), we remain committed to our belief in the importance of leadership in our quest for schools that serve the public purpose. It is in the development and support of the kinds of virtues, skills, and dispositions that are necessary for a healthy democracy that we translate hope for a brighter future for everyone into actions leading toward that future. In this way, we learn from and improve upon the past.

We quoted Neil Postman earlier in this chapter and believe that his statement is worth repeating: "The question is not, Does or doesn't public schooling create a public? The question is, What kind of public does it create?"[19] Formal and informal leaders of schools, of school districts, of various university departments, and of educator preparation programs create and convince others of their vision for schooling. These visions, stories, or narratives often result in actions that can improve, stagnate, or damage our schools. The lesson is a simple one, its enactment is not: The stories we as educators tell must be compelling. They must persuade others that all schools can be good schools and that a good education for everyone has to be a real national priority.

Chapter Eight

Experiencing the Agenda

It may be true that understanding and participating in democracy is, in no small measure, based on engagement with the written word, as Neil Postman has argued.[1] But written or otherwise, language alone is not enough to sustain a democratic way of life. We must also be skilled at translating our understanding and appreciation of democracy into patterns of behavior, whether in the social or the political sphere. It is one thing to know the freedoms that are supposed to be protected by the First Amendment of the U.S. Constitution. It is quite another to recognize when and where they are being violated—and a step further to adopt a public stance of intervention and protest.

Our experiences in implementing the Agenda for Education in a Democracy have, by and large, been quite positive. Nobody has claimed our efforts to be wrongheaded. In fact, the response has been quite the opposite—and herein lies a problem. For most people in the United States, democracy ranks right up there with motherhood and apple pie in the hierarchy of treasured Americana. Democracy is something we count on for our well-being. It takes care of us, nurtures us.

Earlier we talked about the roles played by narratives (some prefer the word *stories*) in the conduct of human affairs. It is narratives, of a sort, that give individuals, communities, and nations a sense of their history as well as lending guidance into unknown futures. These narratives are educative; they transmit elements of a given culture. The stories of immigrants coming to the United States have provided not only an incredible literature but also vivid pictures of sharply contrasting cultures. The passage of these narratives into the larger cultural surround provides contrast, even dissonance, which invigorates the culture into which they have come. Recognition of the great value of diversity to learning and democracy played a vital role in the 2003 Supreme Court decision regarding admissions to the law school of the University of Michigan. (The controversial legal decision attempted to distinguish between the value of diversity and the danger of quotas.)

In the process of enculturating the young, a major responsibility of education is to host and even to fuel debate over what aspects of a culture ought to be preserved. Patriotism that is blind to the inequities, injustices, and threats to freedoms—such as those of speech, the press, and religion—undermines the democratic work-in-progress to which we proclaim allegiance. Had this been the only form of patriotism in our nation's recent past, women would not yet be allowed to vote and our "common" schools would be far more segregated than they are today.

If our democracy is to continue to work toward translating ideals into realities, then these ideals must be embedded in a narrative that guides both the substance and conduct of its schools. In other words, the education necessary to the advancement of democracy must be made safe from the same ills that threaten democracy itself.

Arguably, the greatest of these ills is the complacency inherent in the too-common assumption that democracy is self-perpetuating. Consequently, we need to be at least as engaged in inquiry into democracy as a concept, and into our experience with it, as we are in praising it. Perhaps complacency is not quite the right word, because it implies a recognition of things to be improved that is devoid of the will to do something about them. The real problem seems to be more along the lines of a lack of awareness.

Another ill is that of viewing democracy only as a form of government, taking place primarily in state and federal institutions. Voting often seems to be all that is required of us. But the use and abuse of democratic principles is embedded in how we interact with one another every day of our lives. The basic tenets of social and political democracy are not merely abstractions. Our values, beliefs, actions, and behaviors make them very concrete.

This chapter revisits the mission, conditions, and strategies of the Agenda for Education in a Democracy, primarily as it has played out over the past fifteen years in the National Network for Educational Renewal (NNER). There are two major and con-nected foci: the interplay of individuals and their institutions, and the accompanying alignment and realignment of beliefs, values, and practices. This duality of interplay and alignment is not just one of involving educators from differing professional cultures in learning to work together. It also requires revising or even giving up certain long-established regularities, as well as taking on new ones. Reform usually calls for doing the familiar better; renewal invariably involves letting go of at least some of the familiar.

The domain of inquiry is, of course, education for democracy as played out in schools and in the education of educators for those schools. But as we said earlier, we believe the Agenda to be rele-vant, with appropriate changes in specifics, for the entire panoply of educating that shapes our democracy. Our system of public schooling plays a unique role in creating a democratic public—a role that is necessary but not alone sufficient.

Language and Concepts

Schools have honed their systems and structures while being pushed this way and that by successive eras of reform. Words such as *aims*, *purposes*, *functions*, *principles*, *basics*, *fundamentals*, *excel-lence*, *accountability*, *outcomes*, and the like provide a well-worn vocabulary that constitutes a sort of armor against change. It is almost impossible to avoid repeating them. Nevertheless, we searched for less-used alternatives to draw attention to connota-tions differing from convention. Unfortunately, the need for expla-nation and repetition tends to push the language of fresh concepts toward becoming vocabulary for the old. But at least the effort stimulated vigorous conversation, debate, and some of the subsequent action.

Participants in the Institute for Educational Inquiry's (IEI) Leadership Associates Program (described in Chapter Seven), separated from their places of daily work, were able to concentrate for long, uninterrupted hours on the Agenda and its relationships to this work. It was fascinating to observe the nuances of their fresh insights into familiar concepts that had been little discussed with colleagues back home in their settings. The idea of education as a moral endeavor—but with the word *education* itself as neutral—was intriguing to some who professed to using it commonly to convey only something good, even though they were aware that there could be such a thing as bad education.

Several years after experiencing the program, a political scientist who taught a course on American government spoke of having once assumed our government to be democratic, but later coming to realize that this wasn't always so and that there are deep understandings about democracy itself that must be acquired. As pointed out in *Developing Democratic Character in the Young*, both democracy and education are complex concepts.[2] Try to connect the two and the complexities compound.

In what follows we highlight some of the language and concepts constituting the narrative of the Agenda that have provoked lively conversation and debate not only in our Leadership Associates Program but also in the ongoing work of the NNER. In doing so, we occasionally cite publications that explore these words and concepts in greater depth.[3]

Mission

The creators of the Agenda for Education in a Democracy chose the word *mission* for one of its three major components to try to get around the linearity of means being justified by ends. Mission encompasses values that characterize both ends and means. One might browbeat a child into robotlike behavior that charms the neighbors, but the means employed are immoral. Unpacking the meaning of a democratic educational mission should reveal the principles to be transplanted into the conditions necessary to advance the mission. These principles should in turn characterize the processes of putting the conditions in place. This is not an easy alignment to effect.

Interestingly, at the same time in the early 1990s, that we were endeavoring to develop the necessary understanding and to bring off this alignment within the NNER, schools and school districts across the country were beginning to develop and disseminate their own mission statements. Most of these statements stressed the importance of providing a delivery system for student learning. This is a mechanism—a necessary one—but not a mission. The issue of values guiding this system was neglected.

During the concluding years of the twentieth century and continuing into the twenty-first century, much federal intervention in school practices has emphasized "what works." Little has been said about what works *and is also good*—good in the sense of contributing to a moral mission. Narrowing the focus of standardized tests to accommodate the validity and reliability of assessment begets excessive drill. Some learning should become automatic. But there is no evidence to indicate that performing well on these tests translates into gaining the understandings, skills, and dispositions one needs for living effectively in our world.

Educators working daily in a context of having to justify what they do on the basis of the criterion of narrowly defined outcomes usually have little difficulty recognizing the educational necessity of going far beyond such outcomes in their teaching. Nonetheless, the concept of a moral mission encompassing both ends and means has proven to be a challenging one to fully grasp and then implement in an environment of quite different expectations for schooling.

Moral

Of the trilogy of books based on the Study of the Education of Educators published in 1990, *The Moral Dimensions of Teaching* probably had—and continues to have—the deepest and widest impact.[4] We have been told of spirited conversations about its contents taking place in such different cities as Moscow and Buenos Aires. Reviewers have paid special attention to the book's focus on education and teaching as moral endeavors. Advocacy of "family values" entered the debate of federal elections, and some religious groups thought we might be in favor of prayer in the schools. Others raised questions about what and whose morals we favored. Some even expected the book to be about drugs, alcohol, and extramarital sex.

The readings accompanying discourse in the IEI Leadership Associates Program, including *The Moral Dimensions of Teaching*, sought to answer such questions. The study of education—a very large part of graduate programs for educators—in recent years has emphasized theory and research. These are a big part of our work as well. Consequently, some participants have expected to find in the major studies that contributed to the Agenda some empirical verification—perhaps controlled experimental comparisons—of alternative moral dimensions of education and teaching. But we were not able to provide it. What we found instead was, for the most part, a widespread absence of a clear moral grounding for our formal educational enterprise.

As we said in Chapter One, societies have, over the centuries, engaged in various educational exercises designed to perpetuate beliefs and customs deemed essential to their survival. Some of these beliefs and customs are shed over time, and new ones take hold. The process is evolutionary. What is discarded and what is embraced are not the result of scientific experiments. Similarly, what we propose for education in democracy is grounded in what we have come to understand to be the ideals of the story-in-the-making of democracy itself. These are what we regard as the Agenda's moral grounding.

These democratic political ideals are derived in part from those embedded in the documents that shape and guide the republic that is the United States of America. But both the political and the social are derived from the thinking of rather extraordinary and even wise people—philosophers, political theorists, theologians, economists, paleontologists, historians, and others—who have helped define the moral concepts and principles they have believed are necessary to the well-being of humankind.

Perhaps there is a word in a language other than English that encompasses the sum of these ideals, but we are unaware of it. The best we have come up with to embrace such moral concepts as compassion, civility, civicness, equality, fairness, freedom, and justice is *democracy*.[5] But its usefulness in this regard is acquired only if our understanding of the word extends beyond formal governance to include *all* human associations.

We argue the moral grounding of the Agenda from the perspective of first principles. The concept of their universality has been much discussed in the conversations that are part of experiencing the Agenda. While there are certainly participants who would feel more comfortable with a vast, all-encompassing theory fortified by scientific testing of meticulous hypotheses, we know of no such theory we can offer them. Theories to guide learning, teaching, curriculum development, and the like abound, and choices among these are part of the ongoing discourse and action encompassed by the Agenda. And none of them is free of controversy. But this should not be taken to mean that we are adrift without a compass. As, for example, Kenneth Sirotnik observes in *The Moral Dimensions of Teaching*, no "critics of universal principles of social justice . . . would endorse or even negotiate a new conception of 'justice' based on racial determinism, hedonism, nihilism, or no ethical stance whatsoever."[6]

Sirotnik follows this comment with several sentences (quoted earlier in Chapter Three) that bear repeating because they summarize, in a few choice words, a democratic narrative that answers a number of the questions most often asked about the moral grounding of the Agenda:

> America is a collection of multiple communities defined by different interests, races, ethnicities, regions, economic stratifications, religions, and so forth. Celebrating these differences is part of what makes this nation great. But there is a community—a moral community—that transcends the special interests of individuals, families, groups, that stands for what this nation is all about: liberty *and justice* for all. This "community," of course, is an abstraction. It is a "moral ecology" held together by a political democracy and the fundamental values embedded in the system.[7]

Our system of public schooling is the *only* mechanism we now have for ensuring the apprenticeship in liberty and justice that is necessary to democratic citizenship.

Conversation

In our work we have drawn on the insights of many people, some cited in this manuscript, some in other books we have written. In 2003 we lost another of those great teachers whose quintessential intelligence transcended the boundaries of conventional thought to give us greater understanding of the marvelous complexities of the evolution of human civilizations. Fortunately, Stephen Jay Gould has left us with a breathtaking legacy to draw on for years to come. In the foreword to Gould's collection of essays on baseball (yes, baseball), David Halberstam writes of this icon: "Technically he was a paleontologist, which meant to most of his fellow citizens that he was in the dinosaur business, but I thought of him operating under a broader mandate as a kind of all-purpose historian-detective, working on a span of time which covered a mere three and a half billion years."[8]

On the following page, what Halberstam writes can serve as well to lend clarity to some of our experiences with the Agenda and to remind us of the range of readings we have drawn on to enlighten our thinking about the big ideas of education and democracy and about the assumed "little things" to look for in practice lest we stumble:

> [Gould] was the least narrow of intellectuals: what made his intellect so admirable was his ability to connect seemingly separate developments and truths in one field to developments in another: he could connect dots where few of his colleagues could even see the dots, let alone relate them. . . . He could take big ideas and, through his skills as analyst and writer, make them small, thereby making their truths infinitely more accessible. Equally important, he was capable of taking what were seemingly small truths and, through the proper interpretation, making them large, imbuing them with an importance and a dimension they otherwise lacked.[9]

Many of Gould's connections lie at the very heart of the Agenda. His prize-winning book *The Mismeasure of Man* (one of some thirty he wrote in his too-short life) draws on hard data to debunk the biological determinism that has too long been used to "authenticate" opinions formed out of prejudice and fear. By the mid-1880s, for example, a bevy of anthropologists and psychologists had established the argument that the larger cranium of white males over that of women and black males warranted higher expectations and greater investment for the education of white men. In 1881, one "scientist" savaged women and black men simultaneously: "Men of the black races have a brain scarcely heavier than that of white women."[10]

Note the irony in the use of "Man" in Gould's title—apt in view of the fact that men were doing the measuring to prove the mental superiority of men—and the wry humor in his observation that "[m]illions of people are now suspecting that their social prejudices are scientific facts after all."[11] The practice is alive and well today.

The late historian Lawrence Cremin once asked and then answered the question, "What do we do when faced with tough problems? We talk." But for some, talk simply gets in the way of "expediency." School reform commonly changes the word sequence in "ready, aim, fire" to "fire, aim, ready." Many people tout the concept "Don't stand there; do something"; but in truth, in dealing with most of our problems, especially those that have been with us for a long time, we would be far better advised to sit down and talk—and talk seriously, honestly, and caringly.

In our work we address conversation as a guiding force—to be pursued much like an art form—in our daily lives and in human and natural affairs writ large. Indeed, our major initiative in the arts (in teaching and teacher education) has taught us much about the democratization of teaching through the democratization of conversation. We endeavored to make the big ideas of the human conversation more accessible and to raise the little ideas of ongoing practice to a level befitting their importance in education. An essay about the life and work of philosopher Michael Oakeshott helped us immensely at both levels.[12]

Since 1992, we have used the piece written by Josiah Auspitz soon after Oakeshott's death that appeared in the *American Scholar* in the opening sessions of successive groups of participants in the IEI Leadership Associates Program. This article has served three purposes simultaneously. First, because (as anticipated) nobody in any group had read it before, it established at the outset considerable equity in the conversations of very diverse participants. Nobody had the benefit of a head start. Indeed, nobody appeared to know enough about Oakeshott to awe new colleagues with a high level of discourse regarding his work. Second, there is enough in the Auspitz piece to demonstrate Oakshott's use of conversation, especially around a text, as a pedagogical device. Third, this memorial to the distinguished British philosopher introduced participants to his idea of the human conversation. Consequently, through this one article, we were able to call attention to conversation as a device for addressing the immediacy of the Agenda in our professional lives in the context of the universality of its democratic mission.

The idea of there being one human conversation about family, community, work, play, triumph, tragedy, and hope proved, not surprisingly, to be controversial. Nonetheless, it did move us toward recognition of the commonalities among the world's people. Recognition and acceptance of the commonalities and connectedness among humankind, as one people, could help eliminate much of the struggle toward equity and justice for all. The overwhelming tragedy in the history of civilization has been and continues to be our chronic inability to get along without caste systems. Their presence among birds and other animals, too, suggests that caste may be endemic in the culture of most living things. Clearly, the challenges to education for democracy will be with us into an indefinite future.

Most of us think of conversation as only an oral activity. In the curriculum of the Leadership Associates Program, sessions with senior fellows of the IEI were billed as "conversations" with James Comer, Howard Gardner, Linda Darling-Hammond, Donna Kerr, Theodore Sizer, or another person from this distinguished group. Some participants were puzzled by the designation, observing that some of these were lectures followed by questions. This provided the opportunity to point out that presumably one carries on a silent conversation with a speaker, a book, a movie: "I wonder what she meant by that" or "I disagree" or "I hadn't thought of that before" or "Perhaps I should read that chapter again." One of the shortcomings of distance learning, relieved somewhat by interactive television, is that one misses the body language that may say more about the views of members of a discussion group than does their spoken language.

It has been difficult to convey the strategic purpose of the conversation just described to people who have not experienced it. It is much more than providing satisfying explorations of ideas. The overarching purpose is to foster in participants and their home settings a culture of inquiry, planning, action, and assessment guided by a common mission. Earlier in this book we described our comprehensive study of educational change in which we promoted in eighteen schools a systematic strategy of dialogue, decisions, actions, and evaluation (DDAE) as cultural norms.[13]

In a companion manuscript, one of us has described the boundary-breaking renewal in two very different schools that refined this process over a period of years: one a small school in an isolated rural community with rather low parental expectations for schooling, and the other in a highly literate suburban sector of a large city where the educational expectations of parents were very high.[14] In both schools, the culture, closely linked to its parental community, became the center of renewal. In both, work was carried out at a high level of intellectual discourse closely connected to practice.

Increasingly we have come to see this cultural norm in the most renewing settings of the NNER. The conversations of leadership programs serve as a generator—the beat of a different drummer—but the culture of the individual settings is the institutional agency of change. We could fill a good-sized volume with the case studies of individuals who significantly changed their educational practices as a result of carefully reflecting on their conversational experiences.

Simultaneous Renewal

One self-defeating characteristic of school reform is that of universal relevance. It is like an over-the-counter pill designed to target certain symptoms, but without a proper diagnosis of the ailment. Presumably, if directions are properly followed, the pill will have the desired effect. So one takes the pill and, whether the symptoms go away or not, no changes are made in the behaviors affecting one's health. The recurrence of symptoms—or the onset of new ones—of course leads to taking more pills. So it is with eras of school reform.

The differences between school reform and school renewal are much like the old adage that there is a big difference between giving a man a fish and teaching him to fish. Whereas school reform attempts to include in daily educational fare something that presumably was not there before, school renewal creates an environment—a whole culture—that routinely conducts diagnoses to determine what is going well and what is not. The locus of power and influence shifts dramatically. Opportunities arise to capitalize on what's already working and to build on current successes, to zero in on those areas in need of particular attention, and to formulate and pursue over time a vision of what an institution might be.

The most difficulty we have had and still have with educational renewal as a strategy of planned change has grown out of our use of the adjective *simultaneous*. In the first iteration of the NNER (1986–1990), the representatives of higher education were surprisingly eager to embark on a crusade of improving the K–12 partner schools. Most were little inspired to engage in renewing their own institutional programs of teacher education. Some said they had already done that. Some of the school-based folks were delighted with the prospect and increasing frequency of having the university folks around and engaging in conversation with them. They opened their schools more widely to student teachers from the partnering college or university. But the idea that these student teachers needed to be involved in renewing, innovative practices rather than just adhering to the conventional was much less attractive.

In brief, during the 1990s, school-university partnerships became almost a politically correct idea. *Partnering* was an "in" word. But it became close to a nonevent when studies began to show that positive symbioses were rarely occurring. Such symbioses require recognition by both sets of partners that each has something the other lacks or has little of but would benefit from getting. Positive symbiosis also requires commitment to ensuring that the other party gains what it seeks from the partnership.

The concept of simultaneous renewal is a cornerstone in the work of advancing the Agenda. It is part of the litany of ongoing conversation. It has proved to be a powerful strategy for both building morale and effecting change. But it is exceedingly difficult to sustain. Fortunately, ongoing assessment of implementation keeps simultaneous renewal high on the operational agenda of both participating institutions and their partnering infrastructure.

Postulates

Postulate is one of several rather archaic words we use to provide an intellectual orientation that is somewhat uncommon to an enterprise more accustomed to setting educational objectives as the end, and frequently the means, of educational improvement. There is nothing complex in its definition: a carefully reasoned argument or set of presuppositions. Our postulates (see the Appendix) were derived from not finding in our research on schooling and teacher education conditions that a little thought would reveal to be highly relevant, if not necessary, to the robust conduct of both.

The mission of the Agenda is, as it should be, the challenge to provide in our schools a major part of the educational infrastructure necessary for sustaining and continually improving the health of our social and political democracy. Putting in place the conditions necessary to the education of the nation's teachers and the health of the public schools is a relatively straightforward enterprise warranting the commitment and support we routinely give to much less important components of democracy.

It is time we put behind us mandate-driven school reform initiatives conjured up by political leaders, often at the behest of the corporate community. Presumably, the schools belong to the people, just as do our roads, parks, airwaves, and public services. But again and again those in power ignore what the people expect from their schools and what they might be willing to do and give to realize those expectations. As we stated in Chapter Four, the god of Economic Utility must be forever banished from school policy and practice.

Tomorrow

There exists no tomorrow, as Stewart Brand's *Clock of the Long Now* makes clear.[15] Nobody lives there or has been there. Our stance on tomorrow can only be contemplative. The subjects of our contemplation—issues, problems, work to do, hopes—are already known to us. When the tomorrow we contemplate is suddenly today, our circumstances (barring unpredictable catastrophe) are remarkably familiar.

This is one reason why we know that the Agenda for Education in a Democracy will be relevant when tomorrow becomes today. But there is another reason as well. The major educational and engineering problems of preserving the strengths of a culture and dispensing with its weaknesses have been with us throughout the history of civilization. They will be here when the actual Clock of the Long Now (being constructed in Nevada) tolls the end of one millennium and our entry into another. What we do between now and then will determine whether humans are even there, let alone free to continue the processes of renewal. There is nothing in democracy that ensures its existence when the abstraction of each tomorrow becomes the reality of each today. Democracy is a human-dependent phenomenon.

We said in Chapter Two that the mission of the Agenda has four parts. Two of these parts provide the guiding narrative of schooling: enculturating the young into our social and political democracy, and ensuring the knowledge and dispositions necessary for participating widely and critically in the human conversation. The education that educators receive must prepare them for advancing this mission in the education of children and youths.

But teachers of the young, especially of students in schools, must also educate themselves in the other two elements of the Agenda's mission: sound pedagogy and the moral conduct of the particular enterprise or institution they represent. Teachers are schooling's moral stewards. For further emphasis, we have found it important to add the adjective *caring* to *teaching* and *stewardship*, even though caring should be assumed as a given in both.

In our work—writing, teaching, conferring, conversing, sponsoring initiatives conducted in settings of the NNER, and the rest— we have focused primarily on democracy, education, and the relationship between the two. Because these are the primary sources from which the Agenda's moral grounding has been derived, and because this moral grounding is to be virtually ubiquitous in the conditions and strategies called for in seeking to advance the Agenda's mission, this imbalance probably is desirable. Also, the terrain of curricula, pedagogy, change, and the like that is plowed in implementing the Agenda is very familiar ground for educators. It is making development of democratic character in the young a major guiding narrative in the context of their work that presents the real challenge.

Education for democracy is so essential to our collective well-being that it will remain center stage for us into an indefinite future. We will continue, then, to emphasize the moral ecology of which all of us are a part as we critique the expectations and conditions that seek and often demand entry into the educational institutions upon which the health of this ecology depends. We will elevate in our priorities the curricula, pedagogy, and stewardship—the second, third, and fourth components of the four-part mission—necessary for the well-being of these institutions. And we will endeavor to expand our efforts, particularly through our initiative with selected journalists nationwide to increase public awareness of the critical importance of our schools in the continuing renewal of democracy. As we emphasized earlier, local schools must play a major role in educating everyone about the freedoms and responsibilities of a democratic public.

The new version of the Leadership Associates Program being pilot tested at the time of this writing is geared to these priorities. Participants will continue to be recommended by their home settings on the assumption that they will provide the innovative, visionary leadership described by Howard Gardner in Chapter Seven. And the program will give increased attention to the public context necessary to democratic schools and democratic education.

Replacing Regularities

A formidable ethos of stubborn contrariness encompasses efforts to effect major change in schools and most other institutions. The prevailing cultures of these institutions have an incredible capacity to resist or smother intrusions and derail internal mechanisms for renewal, in spite of a formidable literature of analyses and resulting recommendations for addressing this ethos, based on studies of most fields of human endeavor. These analyses tend to be ignored by reformers, largely because the strategies proposed are necessarily complex and time-consuming. They are, however, highly relevant to processes of renewal, but awareness does not in itself clear paths to change.

This ethos of institutional resistance to change commonly experiences an ambiguous relationship to the ethos of its public surround—its community of varied interests and relationships. This community usually wants its interests better served but not necessarily through changes in the familiar ways. People may want a human being to answer the phone at the local branch of their bank, but they're more likely to get yet another telephone answering software upgrade.

Corporations have the resources to teach the public what to want and to convince people that they *need* what they want. Prospective buyers may not intend to travel the terrain that the SUV in the TV advertisement does, but they want that SUV anyway. Such means of persuasion are not available to change agents in schooling. So the obvious strategy is for school people and their primary clients to join together in the change process. But neither group has sufficient discretionary time. Consequently, mission-oriented educators must take the lead in keeping in close communication with the school's patrons.

In doing so, at least two major ironies arise. First, the ship of schooling must be kept afloat while its programs are being retrofitted. Releasing students early in the day to give teachers the time they need for overhauling school practices is more annoying for most parents than telemarketing calls at dinnertime. Second, if school personnel are able to effect more than cosmetic changes—perhaps by meeting on weekends—they must still find ways to involve parents in understanding the what and the why or they will meet resistance. Scheduling more than an occasional evening is difficult.

One example of the first irony is revealed by a call one of us received from a professor at the University of Washington who sought advice regarding his negative reaction to an organizational change in his daughter's school. He had visited her class and was dismayed over what he considered to be sloppy execution of the plan to promote collaboration among the staff, including team teaching. Persuaded that there might be some merits in the change, he wanted to know why the teachers were not properly prepared to effect it. He was surprised to learn that there were only a couple of days for staff development built into the district's annual budget.

Regarding the second irony, some critics of our public schools and some policymakers have jumped on colleges of education—their prime culprit in such villainy—because a recent report of Public Agenda revealed a disconnect between what these colleges presumably are teaching teachers and what parents and policy-makers say they should be teaching.[16] Now, how are we to interpret the implications of this charge? Are schools of education, unlike schools of engineering, law, and medicine, to draw on only the conventional wisdom as the source of what they teach? Or are schools of education to be held accountable for raising the level of the conventional wisdom, and especially the wisdom of policy-makers, so as to remedy this disconnect?

The longstanding, deep structure of schooling creates conditions (as discussed in Chapter Six) that have caused educational historians, among others, to observe that a school is a school is a school. The need for change is chronic, but there is enough public support for some of those deeply entrenched regularities to make them nearly sacred. To effect change commonly means retaining the sacred and adding the new. This is not renewal.

We must continue to refine processes so that they steadily change what exists into what was envisioned, without creating a schism between what is here today but was not quite here yesterday. To put down yesterday's realities is to bring on their defenders. To have to always defend the new against the old is to make school stewardship a wearying enterprise.

We cringe whenever the Agenda is referred to as a project. Projects usually produce add-ons that, once in place, demand of somebody additional time and attention lest they wither. Work in our culture often seems to take up all available time, the good work no more than the less good.

Whether in reform or renewal, there is inevitably a period when retaining the old regularities while considering the new ones crowds finite time. If that period is prolonged, both old and new suffer and enthusiasm fades. This is why the question of what can and should be shed is as important as what we must do to implement the new vision. Thoughtful dialogue invariably discloses unnecessary routines that can readily be dropped and will rarely be missed. In the change process, few things sustain enthusiasm more than seeing how much space for the new is created by getting rid of what has become old baggage. This is a process to which we need to pay more attention as we continue to build the Agenda into schools and educator preparation programs. There is still a lot of unnecessary baggage wearing out its carriers.

Curricula

The curricular baggage invites work far beyond what can even be summarized here. Once upon a time, a school curriculum hardened into place that which was updated only from time to time and rarely adjusted to the expanding expectations of the cultural surround. There ensued, of course, ideological debate over what the curriculum of schooling should be. This has almost always roiled the waters and changed the balance among the curricular pieces, but the deep structure remains. Good ideas are brought back to life and embellished, but they rarely influence more than a few innovative settings—and usually for only a short time.

Although we would expect this nineteenth-century block of concrete to be honed to the point of having a smooth patina, it remains rough and fragmented. Based largely on a theory of how best to discipline the mind, the academic curriculum required for its exemplary development has declined with the prodigious increase in the numbers of students experiencing it. Given the longstanding neglect of teacher education and the necessity of elementary school teachers to address the whole of curriculum, it is not surprising that some specialists in the academic fields of higher education would prefer that students come to them without having had previous encounters with their disciplines.

Meanwhile, a body of research on cognition has revealed that this curricular block—too generously referred to as academic and basic—does not ground our students who appear to do well with it in the understandings and behaviors required of them in the world outside of schools. Even college graduates who took ample science, statistics, and math courses can confound their employers with their inexactitude in transferring the principles studied to work contexts. It should not surprise us, then, that the behavioral characteristics the Agenda associates with democratic character are quite evenly distributed among members of the populace regardless of their performance on academic tests. Something appears to be either absent in the curriculum of schooling or poorly executed, or both.

There is little in current school reform efforts to give us even a sliver of hope that these troubling circumstances are likely to change. The idea of clear standards and high performance expectations makes rhetorical sense. But there is nothing in the mechanisms of implementation being thrust upon our schools that is likely to internalize these standards in the behavioral repertoire of the young. Indeed, the accompanying cycle of testing and the pressures of accountability—in sharp contrast to educating for individual and collective responsibility—are likely to have precisely the opposite effects.

We are endeavoring to flesh out and to pilot inclusion in elementary and secondary schooling curricular foci drawn directly from the human conversation that envelops all of us, every day—the young included. These foci would not replace the academic subjects; rather, they would draw on them, as Stephen Jay Gould used baseball and Wendell Berry uses our natural habitat as the curricular organizing centers for addressing central themes of human existence.

Conducting schools in a democratic mode presents us with a somewhat lesser challenge than developing democratic citizens. But the apprenticeship in liberty we have discussed in these pages requires major curricular revisions, and it requires teaching of a different order. Neither the curriculum nor the pedagogical revisions needed are new. They simply have not been able to gain significant entry into deep structures of schooling that hardened into place many years ago.

Pedagogy

The art and science of teaching are at the core of good education wherever it exists. Pedagogy is the DNA embedded in the biological system of the career teacher. Perhaps this is why it has escaped definitive diagnosis and how-to-do-it formulae. David Solway writes that teaching methods of teaching is an abomination—and that "the only indispensable audiovisual 'device' is the teacher himself."[17] N. L. Gage, in a sweeping review of the literature up to just about three decades ago, saw no diminution of the need for artistry in teaching. He also sounded an optimistic note, writing that "steadily improving connections between teaching patterns and educational outcomes will become more useful tools in the war against ignorance and alienation."[18]

Gage probably would agree with Solway's observation "that the marrow-nature of teaching is the creation of an atmosphere of intellectual reciprocity and enthusiasm, the building of conviction, the evocation of an attitude or a state of mind."[19] But they would disagree on how to create that atmosphere and how to prepare a teacher for doing so. A substantive inquiry into both sets of actions has occurred since these writings appeared, but there has been little to settle the disagreement. The art and science of teaching present a slippery slope of study. A lot of debris lies at its bottom.

We have used and experienced in our Leadership Associates Program and beyond a wide array of pedagogical approaches. The conversational one described earlier, commonly built around some kind of text, has created pervasive intellectual reciprocity and has evoked, we think, much of the state of mind hoped for in experiencing the Agenda.

These conversations are designed to serve as a bridge to participants' teaching back home, and they strive to connect directly to the classroom experiences of their students—be they in elementary or secondary schools or in educator preparation programs. Postulate Ten in particular speaks to this connection, stating, "Programs for the education of educators must be characterized in all respects by the conditions for learning that future teachers are to establish in their own schools and classrooms." We have made a quite demanding commitment to abide by this pedagogical presupposition—a presupposition of our own making. Awareness of this commitment among those who join us from diverse settings across the country may be one of our most powerful teaching allies.

An old and too much ignored lesson in teaching is to connect with the intended learner's present beliefs and knowledge. We would broaden this to include as much as possible of the learner's context. The overloading of students and the prescription of curricula in most of today's educational settings sharply curtail teachers' ability to effect this personal connection. It should not surprise us, then, that these circumstances contribute significantly to the disconnect between schooling and daily life. Nor should we be surprised that gaining credentials has supplanted getting a broad and deep general education as motivation for going to college.

It is to these circumstances—"trappings" might be a more evocative word—in addition to curricula and pedagogy that those of us endeavoring to implement the Agenda will continue to address our attention. We will enjoy the company of other agencies and groups that seek smaller, more intimate schools; fewer daily classes conducted over longer periods; much reduction leading to the elimination of students boxed into age- and grade-level learning; artful blending of human and technological energy systems into the teacher-learner relationship; redesign of the formal educational apparatus to conform more closely with what we know about human development and learning; and especially our core work of educating the young in the qualities of democratic citizenship and keeping democracy safe for the conduct of this educational apprenticeship.

An old adage admonishes physicians to "heal thyself." For us, another might well be "know thy limitations." We think we do. So we choose carefully among the many enticements to do good work. This is not easy, because our top priorities often are not initiatives that fit nicely into the priorities of potential sources of financial support. It is more than a little disconcerting to be told that, yes, developing democratic schools is important, but it does not raise test scores and therefore is not deserving of funding at this time.

Our sustaining hope is that the current dreary era of school reform will soon end. Meanwhile, the need to take care of our democracy, as we would have it take care of us, grows more and more urgent and apparent. A sustaining motivation stems from the message of democracy itself being one of hope.[20] To be at once an educator and a pessimist regarding the future of the human race is the ultimate oxymoron.

Notes

Chapter One

1. Alicja Iwańska, "The Role of the Curriculum Maker in Cross-National Perspective," in *Curriculum Inquiry*, J. I. Goodlad and Associates (New York: McGraw-Hill, 1979), 246.
2. Mortimer J. Adler, *The Paideia Proposal* (New York: Macmillan, 1982), v.
3. Iwańska, "The Role of the Curriculum Maker," 246. For a critique of Skinner's book *Walden Two* and of utopian conceptions generally, see Seymour B. Sarason's *The Creation of Settings and the Future Societies* (San Francisco: Jossey-Bass, 1972), esp. chap. 12.
4. Nothing is more critical to the well-being of a culture than its development of the wisdom to preserve what is essential to its well-being—a classic curricular issue. For a comprehensive examination of this issue, see Jane Roland Martin, *Cultural Miseducation: In Search of a Democratic Solution* (New York: Teachers College Press, 2002).
5. For a fascinating and controversial account of the emergence and status of childhood over the passage of time, see Philippe Ariès, *Centuries of Childhood*, trans. R. Baldick (New York: Vintage Books, 1962).
6. Gary D Fenstermacher, "Moral Considerations on Teaching as a Profession," in *The Moral Dimensions of Teaching*, ed. J. I. Goodlad, R. Soder, and K. A. Sirotnik (San Francisco: Jossey-Bass, 1990), 133.

7. Lawrence A. Cremin, *Popular Education and Its Discontents* (New York: HarperCollins, 1990).

8. Hal A. Lawson, "Expanding the Goodlad Agenda: Interprofessional Education and Community Collaboration in Service of Vulnerable Children, Youth, and Families," *Holistic Education*, 1996, 9, 20–34.

9. Alexis de Tocqueville, *Democracy in America*, trans. H. Reeve (New York: Vintage, 1945), vol. 1, chap. 14, 256. Vols. 1 and 2 originally published 1835 and 1840, respectively.

10. Benjamin R. Barber, "Public Schooling: Education for Democracy," in *The Public Purpose of Education and Schooling*, ed. J. I. Goodlad and T. J. McMannon (San Francisco: Jossey-Bass, 1997), 29.

11. Benjamin R. Barber, "America Skips School," *Harper's Magazine*, 1993, 286, 46.

12. Kenneth A. Sirotnik and Associates, *Renewing Schools and Teacher Education: An Odyssey in Educational Change* (Washington D.C.: American Association of Colleges for Teacher Education, 2001). Much of the information in this chapter is drawn from this source. Readers seeking a more complete understanding of the subjects introduced here are encouraged to consult Sirotnik's report.

13. John I. Goodlad, "The Reconstruction of Teacher Education," *Teachers College Record*, 1970, 72, 61–72.

14. John I. Goodlad, *A Place Called School: Prospects for the Future* (New York: McGraw-Hill, 1984).

15. Sirotnik, *Renewing Schools and Teacher Education*, 3.

16. National Commission on Excellence in Education, *A Nation at Risk: The Imperative for Educational Reform* (Washington D.C.: U.S. Government Printing Office, 1983).

17. Laboratory in School and Community Education, *Linking Educational Theory and School Practice: The Laboratory in School and Community Education*, Occasional Paper no. 1 (Los Angeles: Laboratory in School and Community Education, 1985), 18.

18. John I. Goodlad, *Educational Renewal: Better Teachers, Better Schools* (San Francisco: Jossey-Bass, 1994), 10.
19. Goodlad, *Educational Renewal*, 10–11.
20. John I. Goodlad, *Teachers for Our Nation's Schools* (San Francisco: Jossey-Bass, 1990), 324–325.

Chapter Two

1. Sirotnik and Associates, *Renewing Schools and Teacher Education*, 13.
2. Goodlad, *A Place Called School*, 48.
3. Goodlad, *Teachers for Our Nation's Schools*, 48.
4. The twenty postulates can be found in the Appendix.
5. Sirotnik and Associates, *Renewing Schools and Teacher Education*, 18.
6. Goodlad, *Teachers for Our Nation's Schools*, 268.
7. Sirotnik and Associates, *Renewing Schools and Teacher Education*, 18.
8. Sirotnik and Associates, *Renewing Schools and Teacher Education*, 19.
9. John I. Goodlad, "School-University Partnerships for Educational Renewal: Rationale and Concepts," in *School-University Partnerships in Action: Concepts, Cases, and Concerns*, ed. K. A. Sirotnik and J. I. Goodlad (New York: Teachers College Press, 1988), 26–27.
10. Sirotnik and Associates, *Renewing Schools and Teacher Education*, 32.
11. Sirotnik and Associates, *Renewing Schools and Teacher Education*, 26.
12. Sirotnik and Associates, *Renewing Schools and Teacher Education*, 26.
13. Goodlad, *Educational Renewal*, 3–4.
14. John I. Goodlad, "The Occupation of Teaching in Schools," in *The Moral Dimensions of Teaching*, ed. J. I. Goodlad, R. Soder, and K. A. Sirotnik (San Francisco: Jossey-Bass, 1990), 19.

15. Goodlad, "The Occupation of Teaching in Schools," 19.
16. Goodlad, "The Occupation of Teaching in Schools," 20.
17. Goodlad, "The Occupation of Teaching in Schools," 20–21.
18. Goodlad, "The Occupation of Teaching in Schools," 21–22.
19. Goodlad, "The Occupation of Teaching in Schools," 22.
20. Goodlad, "The Occupation of Teaching in Schools," 24.
21. Goodlad, "The Occupation of Teaching in Schools," 25–27.
22. Goodlad, "The Occupation of Teaching in Schools," 28.
23. John I. Goodlad, *In Praise of Education* (New York: Teachers College Press, 1997), 23.
24. Goodlad, "The Occupation of Teaching in Schools," 23.

Chapter Three

1. Benjamin R. Barber, "Public Schooling: Education for a Democracy," in *The Public Purpose of Education and Schooling,* ed. J. I. Goodlad and T. J. McMannon (San Francisco: Jossey-Bass, 1997), 22.
2. Barber, "Public Schooling," 26.
3. Robert B. Westbrook, "Public Schooling and American Democracy," in *Democracy, Education, and the Schools,* ed. R. Soder (San Francisco: Jossey-Bass, 1996), 125.
4. Barber, "Public Schooling," 27.
5. Quoted in Kern Alexander and M. David Alexander, *American Public School Law,* 3rd ed. (St. Paul, Minn.: West, 1992), 20.
6. Julie Underwood, "Choice, the American Common School, and Democracy," in *Developing Democratic Character in the Young,* ed. R. Soder, J. I. Goodlad, and T. J. McMannon (San Francisco: Jossey-Bass, 2001), 172.
7. Roger Soder, "Education for Democracy: The Foundation for Democratic Character," in *Developing Democratic Character in the Young,* ed. R. Soder, J. I. Goodlad, and T. J. McMannon (San Francisco: Jossey-Bass, 2001), 195–196.
8. Soder, "Education for Democracy," 196.

9. Soder, "Education for Democracy," 196–197; John Dewey, "Creative Democracy: The Task Before Us," in *The Later Works, 1925–1953*, vol. 14: *1939–1941*, ed. J. A. Boydston (Carbondale: Southern Illinois University Press, 1988), 227.

10. Soder, "Education for Democracy," 197.

11. Soder, "Education for Democracy," 197.

12. Barber, "Public Schooling," 26–27.

13. Barber, "Public Schooling," 27.

14. Nathan Tarcov, "The Meanings of Democracy," in Democracy, Education, and the Schools, ed. R. Soder (San Francisco: Jossey-Bass, 1996), 25.

15. Tarcov, "The Meanings of Democracy," 25.

16. Tocqueville, *Democracy in America*, vol. 1, chap. 14, 256.

17. Barber, "Public Schooling," 27.

18. Goodlad, *In Praise of Education*, 26.

19. Underwood, "Choice," 177.

20. Underwood, "Choice," 175.

21. Westbrook, "Public Schooling and American Democracy," 125.

22. Goodlad, *In Praise of Education*, 25.

23. Goodlad, *In Praise of Education*, 58.

24. Linda Darling-Hammond and Jacqueline Ancess, "Democracy and Access to Education," in *Democracy, Education, and the Schools*, ed. R. Soder (San Francisco: Jossey-Bass, 1996), 153. For more on Thomas Jefferson's views concerning education in a democratic society, see Gordon C. Lee, "Learning and Liberty: The Jeffersonian Tradition in Education," in *Crusade Against Ignorance: Thomas Jefferson on Education*, ed. G. C. Lee (New York: Columbia University, 1961), 1–26.

25. Darling-Hammond and Ancess, "Democracy and Access to Education," 153.

26. Barry L. Bull, "The Limits of Teacher Professionalization," in *The Moral Dimensions of Teaching*, ed. J. I. Goodlad, R. Soder, and K. A. Sirotnik (San Francisco: Jossey-Bass, 1990), 87–88.

27. Bull, "The Limits of Teacher Professionalization," 90.

28. Alan T. Wood, *What Does It Mean To Be Human?* (New York: Peter Lang, 2001), 1.
29. Wood, *What Does It Mean To Be Human?* 3.
30. Bull, "Limits of Teacher Professionalization," 90.
31. Bull, "Limits of Teacher Professionalization," 101.
32. Benjamin R. Barber, *An Aristocracy of Everyone* (New York: Ballantine Books, 1992), 39.
33. Kenneth A. Sirotnik, "Society, Schooling, Teaching, and Preparing to Teach," in *The Moral Dimensions of Teaching*, ed. J. I. Goodlad, R. Soder, and K. A. Sirotnik (San Francisco: Jossey-Bass, 1990), 307.

Chapter Four

1. Al Haber, "Campus Report," Summer 1961, 4.
2. Neil Postman, *The End of Education: Redefining the Value of School* (New York: Knopf, 1995), 27.
3. Postman, *The End of Education*, 27–28.
4. Postman, *The End of Education*, 28.
5. Postman, *The End of Education*, 32–33. Italics in original.
6. John I. Goodlad, "Kudzu, Rabbits, and School Reform," in *Phi Delta Kappan*, 2002, 84(1), 18.
7. David Halberstam, *The Fifties* (New York: Random House, 1993), 625–626.
8. David Burner, *Making Peace with the Sixties* (Princeton, N.J.: Princeton University Press, 1996), 178.
9. James S. Coleman and others, *Equality of Educational Opportunity* (Washington, D.C.: U.S. Department of Health, Education and Welfare, 1966).
10. Daniel P. Moynihan, *The Negro Family: A Case for National Action* (Washington, D.C.: U.S. Department of Labor, 1965).
11. Francis Fukuyama, *The Great Disruption: Human Nature and the Reconstruction of Social Order* (New York: Free Press, 1999), 115–116.

12. William Ryan, *Blaming the Victim*, rev. and updated. (New York: Random House, 1976), 310. Originally published 1971.
13. Ryan, *Blaming the Victim*, 64.
14. Theodore R. Sizer, "The Meanings of 'Public Education,'" in *The Public Purpose of Education and Schooling*, ed. J. I. Goodlad and T. J. McMannon (San Francisco: Jossey-Bass, 1997), 39.
15. John I. Goodlad, "Elementary Education," in *Education and the Idea of Mankind*, ed. R. Ulich (New York: Harcourt, Brace & World, 1964), 104–105. Data are drawn from the National Society for the Study of Education, *Individualizing Instruction*, Sixty-First Yearbook, Part 1 (Chicago: University of Chicago Press, 1962); and John I. Goodlad, "Classroom Organization," in *Encyclopedia of Educational Research*, ed. Chester W. Harris (New York: Macmillan, 1960), 221–226.
16. Goodlad, *Teachers for Our Nation's Schools*, 2.
17. Roger Soder, "When Words Find Their Meaning: Renewal Versus Reform," in *Phi Delta Kappan*, Apr. 1999, 568.
18. Soder, "When Words Find Their Meaning," 568.
19. Soder, "When Words Find Their Meaning," 569.
20. Soder, "When Words Find Their Meaning," 569.
21. Soder, "When Words Find Their Meaning," 570.
22. John I. Goodlad, "Flow, Eros, and Ethos in Educational Renewal," in *Phi Delta Kappan*, Apr. 1999, 576.
23. Goodlad, "Flow, Eros, and Ethos," 574.
24. Goodlad, "Flow, Eros, and Ethos," 575.
25. Nel Noddings, "Renewing Democracy in Schools," in *Phi Delta Kappan*, Apr. 1999, 580.
26. Walter C. Parker, "Curriculum for Democracy," in *Democracy, Education, and the Schools*, ed. R. Soder (San Francisco: Jossey-Bass, 1996), 182.
27. Sizer, "The Meanings of 'Public Education,'" 40.
28. Linda Darling-Hammond, "Education, Equity, and the Right to Learn," in *The Public Purpose of Education and Schooling*, ed. J. I. Goodlad and T. J. McMannon (San Francisco: Jossey-Bass, 1997), 43–44.

29. John I. Goodlad, "Nourishing an Ecology of Educational Belief," address to the annual meeting of the National Network for Educational Renewal, Parsippany, N.J., Oct. 24, 2002.

Chapter Five

1. Soder, "Education for Democracy," 199.
2. Soder, "Education for Democracy," 199.
3. Goodlad, *In Praise of Education*, 4–5.
4. Todd Gitlin, *Media Unlimited: How the Torrent of Images and Sounds Overwhelms Our Lives* (New York: Henry Holt, 2001), 17–18.
5. Nel Noddings, "Public Schooling, Democracy, and Religious Dissent," in *Developing Democratic Character in the Young*, ed. R. Soder, J. I. Goodlad, and T. J. McMannon (San Francisco: Jossey-Bass, 2001), 165.
6. Barber, *An Aristocracy of Everyone*, 82–83.
7. For an expanded discussion of these ideas, see Mark Johnson's *Moral Imagination: Implications of Cognitive Science for Ethics* (Chicago: University of Chicago Press, 1993).
8. Barber, *An Aristocracy of Everyone*, 83.
9. Goodlad, *In Praise of Education*, 43.
10. Goodlad, *In Praise of Education*, 61.
11. Goodlad, *In Praise of Education*, 62.
12. Barber, *An Aristocracy of Everyone*, 103.
13. Howard Zinn, *A People's History of the United States: 1492— Present*, 20th Anniversary Ed. (New York: HarperCollins, 1999), 658.
14. Zinn, *A People's History*, 658.
15. Neil Postman, *Building a Bridge to the Eighteenth Century* (New York: Knopf, 1999), 101.
16. Postman, *Building a Bridge*, 89–90.
17. Robert D. Putnam, *Bowling Alone: The Collapse and Revival of American Community* (New York: Simon & Schuster, 2000), 46.

18. Deborah Meier, *The Power of Their Ideas: Lessons for America from a Small School in Harlem* (Boston: Beacon Press, 1995), 81.

Chapter Six

1. Compare Paul Berman and Milbrey McLaughlin, *Federal Programs Supporting Educational Change*, Report No. R-1589/7-HEW (Santa Monica, Calif.: Rand Corporation, Sept. 1974); and John I. Goodlad, Francis Klein, and Associates, *Looking Behind the Classroom Door* (Worthington, Ohio: Charles A. Jones, 1974).

2. For a more complete discussion, see Kenneth A. Sirotnik, "The Meaning and Conduct of Inquiry in School-University Partnerships," in *School-University Partnerships in Action: Concepts, Cases, and Concerns*, ed. K. A. Sirotnik and J. I. Goodlad (New York: Teachers College Press, 1988), 175–177. For a detailed description and analysis of renewal extending over a long period in two very different school settings, see chap. 9 in John I. Goodlad's *Romances with Schools* (New York: McGraw-Hill, 2004).

3. John I. Goodlad, *The Dynamics of Educational Change* (New York: McGraw-Hill, 1975), 206. For further discussion, see also Mary M. Bentzen, *Changing Schools: The Magic Feather Principle* (New York: McGraw-Hill, 1974). Both texts draw on work conducted with the League of Cooperating Schools.

4. Goodlad, *Dynamics*, 13.

5. Edward T. Hall, *Beyond Culture* (New York: Anchor Books, 1979), 16–17.

6. Paul Heckman, "Understanding School Culture," in *The Ecology of School Renewal*, Eighty-Sixth Yearbook, Part 1, National Society for the Study of Education, ed. J. I. Goodlad, (Chicago: University of Chicago Press, 1987), 69.

7. Most of these are listed in the publications resulting from the succession of activities. As stated in the Preface, the reports, articles, and books are the sources for the present writing; many are cited in the chapter notes.

8. See Bentzen, *Changing Schools*.

9. John I. Goodlad, *A Place Called School* (New York: McGraw-Hill, 1984); and Goodlad, *Teachers for Our Nation's Schools*.

10. Goodlad, *Educational Renewal*, 1–2.

11. Goodlad, *Dynamics of Educational Change*, 166.

12. Martin Haberman, "Twenty-Three Reasons Why Universities Can't Educate Teachers," in *Journal of Teacher Education*, 22, 134.

13. Goodlad, *Dynamics of Educational Change*, 166.

14. Goodlad, *Educational Renewal*, 2.

15. See Robert S. Patterson, Nicholas M. Michelli, and Arturo Pacheco, *Centers of Pedagogy: New Structures for Educational Renewal* (San Francisco: Jossey-Bass, 1999).

16. See Carnegie Forum on Education and the Economy, *A Nation Prepared: Teachers for the Twenty-First Century* (Washington D.C.: Carnegie Forum on Education and the Economy, 1986); Holmes Group, *Tomorrow's Teachers: A Report of the Holmes Group* (East Lansing, Mich.: Holmes Group, 1986); and Goodlad, *A Place Called School*.

17. Richard W. Clark, *Effective Professional Development Schools* (San Francisco: Jossey-Bass, 1999); and Goodlad, *Educational Renewal*, 96–130.

18. Richard W. Clark and Donna M. Hughes, *Partner Schools: Definitions and Expectations*, rev. ed. (Seattle, Wash.: Center for Educational Renewal, University of Washington, 1995).

19. Corinne Mantle-Bromley, "The Status of Early Theories of Professional Development School Potential in Four Settings Across the United States," in *Forging Alliances in Community and Thought*, ed. I. N. Guadarrama, J. Ramsey, and J. Nath (Greenwich, Conn.: Information Age Publishing, 2002).

20. Paul E. Heckman and Corinne Mantle-Bromley, "Toward Renewal in School-University Partnerships," in *The Teaching Career*, ed. J. I. Goodlad and T. J. McMannon (New York: Teachers College Press, 2004).

21. Heckman and Mantle-Bromley, "Toward Renewal," 7–8.

22. Steve Earle, *Jerusalem*, Artemis Records, 2002.

Chapter Seven

1. Daniel P. Liston and Kenneth M. Zeichner, *Culture and Teaching* (Mahwah, N.J.: Erlbaum, 1996), 85.
2. Howard Gardner, *Leading Minds: An Anatomy of Leadership* (New York: HarperCollins, 1995), 8–9.
3. Postman, *End of Education*, 7.
4. Postman, *End of Education*, 18.
5. Richard W. Clark, *Effective Professional Development Schools* (San Francisco: Jossey-Bass, 1999), 239.
6. Mantle-Bromley, "Status of Early Theories," 3–30.
7. Sirotnik and Associates, *Renewing Schools and Teacher Education*, 177.
8. Gardner, *Leading Minds*, 14.
9. Wilma F. Smith, "Serving as Moral Stewards of the Schools," in *Leadership for Educational Renewal: Developing a Cadre of Leaders*, ed. W. F. Smith and G. D Fenstermacher (San Francisco: Jossey Bass, 1999), 155–185.
10. Robert S. Patterson, Nicholas M. Michelli, and Arturo Pacheco, *Centers of Pedagogy: New Structures for Educational Renewal* (San Francisco: Jossey-Bass, 1999).
11. Clark, *Effective Professional Development Schools*, 240–243.
12. Kay A. Norlander-Case, Timothy G. Reagan, and Charles W. Case, *The Professional Teacher: The Preparation and Nurturance of the Reflective Practitioner* (San Francisco: Jossey-Bass, 1999).
13. Soder, "Education for Democracy," 182–205.
14. Roger Soder, *The Language of Leadership* (San Francisco: Jossey-Bass, 2001), 163.
15. For more on this, see Goodlad, *Teachers for Our Nation's Schools*, 126–132.
16. For more on this, see esp. Parts 1 and 3 of Wilma F. Smith and Gary D Fenstermacher, eds., *Leadership for Educational Renewal: Developing a Cadre of Leaders* (San Francisco: Jossey-Bass, 1999). For discussions of evaluation and impact, see Part 4, as well as Sirotnik's *Renewing Schools and Teacher Education*.

17. This section draws heavily on Wilma Smith's "Developing Leadership for Educational Renewal," in Smith and Fenstermacher's *Leadership for Educational Renewal*, 29–46.

18. Patterson, Michelli, and Pacheco, *Centers of Pedagogy*, 176–177.

19. Postman, *The End of Education*, 7.

Chapter Eight

1. Neil Postman, "Democracy," in *Building a Bridge to the Eighteenth Century: How the Past Can Improve Our Future* (New York: Knopf, 1999), 136–154.

2. Roger Soder, John I. Goodlad, and Timothy J. McMannon, eds., *Developing Democratic Character in the Young* (San Francisco: Jossey-Bass, 2001).

3. Where we have already referred to them elsewhere in the text, such references are not repeated.

4. John I. Goodlad, Roger Soder, and Kenneth A. Sirotnik, eds., *The Moral Dimensions of Teaching* (San Francisco: Jossey-Bass, 1990). The other two books in the trilogy are Goodlad's *Teachers for Our Nation's Schools* and John I. Goodlad, Roger Soder, and Kenneth A. Sirotnik, eds., *Places Where Teachers Are Taught* (San Francisco: Jossey-Bass, 1990).

5. For a more complete discussion of this, see Goodlad's *In Praise of Education*.

6. Goodlad, Soder, and Sirotnik, *Moral Dimensions of Teaching*, 307.

7. Goodlad, Soder, and Sirotnik, *Moral Dimensions of Teaching*, 307.

8. David Halberstam, "Foreword," in Stephen Jay Gould, *Triumph in Tragedy in Mudville* (New York: Norton, 2003), 9.

9. Halberstam, "Foreword," 10.

10. This slighting of women and black men was the work of anthropologist G. Hervé and is cited in Stephen Jay Gould, *The Mismeasure of Man* (New York: Norton, 1981), 35.

11. Gould, *The Mismeasure of Man*, 25.

12. Josiah L. Auspitz had earlier engaged in conversation with Oakeshott. See "Michael Oakeshott: 1901–1990," *American Scholar*, 1991, 60, 351–370.

13. See the discussion of the League of Cooperating Schools in Chapter Six.

14. For case studies of the two schools, see Chapter Nine in Goodlad, *Romances with Schools*.

15. Stewart Brand, *The Clock of the Long Now: Time and Responsibility—The Ideas Behind the World's Slowest Computer* (New York: Basic Books, 1999).

16. Jean Johnson and Ann Duffett, with Jackie Vine and Leslie Moye, *Where We Are Now: Twelve Things You Need to Know About Public Opinion and Public Schools* (New York: Public Agenda, 2003).

17. David Solway, *Education Lost* (Toronto: Ontario Institute for Studies in Education/University of Toronto Press, 1989), 10.

18. Nathaniel Lees Gage, *The Scientific Basis of the Art of Teaching* (New York: Teachers College Press, 1978), 94.

19. Solway, *Education Lost*, 10.

20. See the array of essays in Stephen John Goodlad, *The Last Best Hope: A Democracy Reader* (San Francisco: Jossey-Bass, 2001).

Appendix

The Twenty Postulates Necessary for the Simultaneous Renewal of Schools and the Education of Educators

Postulate One. Programs for the education of the nation's educators must be viewed by institutions offering them as a major responsibility to society and be adequately supported and promoted and vigorously advanced by the institution's top leadership.

Postulate Two. Programs for the education of educators must enjoy parity with other professional education programs, full legitimacy and institutional commitment, and rewards for faculty geared to the nature of the field.

Postulate Three. Programs for the education of educators must be autonomous and secure in their borders, with clear organizational identity, constancy of budget and personnel, and decision-making authority similar to that enjoyed by the major professional schools.

Postulate Four. There must exist a clearly identifiable group of academic and clinical faculty members for whom teacher education is the top priority; the group must be responsible and accountable for selecting diverse groups of students and monitoring their progress, planning and maintaining the full scope and sequence of the curriculum, continuously evaluating and improving programs, and facilitating the entry of graduates into teaching careers.

The first nineteen postulates are from John I. Goodlad, *Educational Renewal: Better Teachers, Better Schools* (San Francisco: Jossey-Bass, 1994), 72–93. Postulate twenty was added in August 2000.

Postulate Five. The responsible group of academic and clinical faculty members described above must have a comprehensive understanding of the aims of education and the role of schools in our society and be fully committed to selecting and preparing teachers to assume the full range of educational responsibilities required.

Postulate Six. The responsible group of academic and clinical faculty members must seek out and select for a predetermined number of student places in the program those candidates who reveal an initial commitment to the moral, ethical, and enculturating responsibilities to be assumed, and make clear to them that preparing for these responsibilities is central to this program.

Postulate Seven. Programs for the education of educators, whether elementary or secondary, must carry the responsibility to ensure that all candidates progressing through them possess or acquire the literacy and critical-thinking abilities associated with the concept of an educated person.

Postulate Eight. Programs for the education of educators must provide extensive opportunities for future teachers to move beyond being students of organized knowledge to become teachers who inquire into both knowledge and its teaching.

Postulate Nine. Programs for the education of educators must be characterized by a socialization process through which candidates transcend their self-oriented student preoccupations to become more other-oriented in identifying with a culture of teaching.

Postulate Ten. Programs for the education of educators must be characterized in all respects by the conditions for learning that future teachers are to establish in their own schools and classrooms.

Postulate Eleven. Programs for the education of educators must be conducted in such a way that future teachers inquire into the nature of teaching and schooling and assume that they will do so as a natural aspect of their careers.

Postulate Twelve. Programs for the education of educators must involve future teachers in the issues and dilemmas that emerge out of the never-ending tension between the rights and interests of individual parents and interest groups and the role of schools in transcending parochialism and advancing community in a democratic society.

Postulate Thirteen. Programs for the education of educators must be infused with understanding of and commitment to the moral obligation of teachers to ensure equitable access to and engagement in the best possible K–12 education for all children and youths.

Postulate Fourteen. Programs for the education of educators must involve future teachers not only in understanding schools as they are but in alternatives, the assumptions underlying alternatives, and how to effect needed changes in school organization, pupil grouping, curriculum, and more.

Postulate Fifteen. Programs for the education of educators must assure for each candidate the availability of a wide array of laboratory settings for simulation, observation, hands-on experiences, and exemplary schools for internships and residencies; they must admit no more students to their programs than can be assured these quality experiences.

Postulate Sixteen. Programs for the education of educators must engage future teachers in the problems and dilemmas arising out of the inevitable conflicts and incongruities between what is perceived to work in practice and the research and theory supporting other options.

Postulate Seventeen. Programs for the education of educators must establish linkages with graduates for purposes of both evaluating and revising these programs and easing the critical early years of transition into teaching.

Postulate Eighteen. Programs for the education of educators require a regulatory context with respect to licensing, certifying, and accrediting that ensures at all times the presence of the necessary conditions embraced by the seventeen preceding postulates.

Postulate Nineteen. Programs for the education of educators must compete in an arena that rewards efforts to continuously improve on the conditions embedded in all of the postulates and tolerates no shortcuts intended to ensure a supply of teachers.

Postulate Twenty. Those institutions and organizations that prepare the nation's teachers, authorize their right to teach, and employ them must fine-tune their individual and collaborative roles to support and sustain lifelong teaching careers characterized by professional growth, service, and satisfaction.

Index